RIGHTING CANADA'S WRONGS

RESOURCE GUIDE

Lindsay Gibson, Ilan Danjoux, and Roland Case
The Critical Thinking Consortium

JAMES LORIMER & COMPANY LTD., PUBLISHERS
TORONTO

James Lorimer & Company Ltd., Publishers acknowledges the support of the Ontario Arts Council. We acknowledge the financial support of the Government of Canada through the Canada Book Fund for our publishing activities. We acknowledge the support of the Canada Council for the Arts, which last year invested $24.3 million in writing and publishing throughout Canada. We acknowledge the Government of Ontario through the Ontario Media Development Corporation's Ontario Book Initiative. We acknowledge the support of the Government of Canada through the Community Historical Recognition Program.

Author Credits: Lindsay Gibson, Ilan Danjoux, and Roland Case for The Critical Thinking Consortium

Cover Image: iStock

Library and Archives Canada Cataloguing in Publication

Gibson, Lindsay, 1975 –
    Righting Canada's wrongs resource guide / Lindsay Gibson, Ilan Danjoux, Roland Case, the Critical Thinking Consortium.

Issued also in electronic format.
ISBN 978-1-4594-0364-2

    1. World War, 1939–945 — Prisoners and prisons, Canadian— Moral and ethical aspects— Juvenile literature. 2. World War, 1939-1945— Moral and ethical aspects— Canada— Juvenile literature. 3. Canada— Moral conditions— History— 20th century— Juvenile literature. 4. Canada— Ethnic relations— History— 20th century— Juvenile literature. I. Case, Roland, 1951– II. Danjoux, Ilan III. Critical Thinking Consortium. IV. Title.

D805.C3G52 2012   j940.53'1771   C2012-906697-4

James Lorimer & Company Ltd., Publishers
317 Adelaide Street West, Suite 1002
Toronto, ON, Canada
M5V 1P9
www.lorimer.ca

Printed and bound in Canada
Manufactured by Marquis

Contents

Introduction

Objectives

In cooperation with The Critical Thinking Consortium we have developed seven lessons for use with books in the Righting Canada's Wrongs series to promote the following objectives:

- **Providing a more complete picture of our past.** The study of Canadian history requires that students don't just learn about the glorious side of our national story. They must also understand the injustices that have knowingly been committed in our history. The message is not one of pessimism, rather it focuses on the ways in which minority groups have been treated in the past; and in many cases, it chronicles stories of dignity, courage, and perseverance, and the triumph of right over wrong.

- **Using engaging primary sources.** The lessons help students make rich use of the abundant variety of primary sources found in each book. These sources include photographs, official documents, letters, political cartoons, and written accounts supplemented by rich textual annotations.

- **Rooting out institutional racism.** The hope is that by building greater awareness of the deep-rooted racist and non-inclusive attitudes of the individuals, groups, and governments behind each of these injustices, we will decrease the likelihood of events or attitudes like these happening again.

- **Teaching historical thinking.** Each lesson supports students in exploring various concepts found in the framework for historical thinking developed by Professor Peter Seixas of the University of British Columbia. www.historicalthinking.ca

Overview of the lessons

Before using any of the other six lessons, we recommend introducing students to the strategies for analyzing photographs and drawings explained in the following lesson:

1. Reading an image

Once students understand how to interpret images, choose one or more of the following six lessons depending on the fit with the curriculum and teachers' objectives:

2. Adopting historical perspectives

3. Tracking continuity and change

4. Examining historical causation

5. Identifying consequences

6. Offering ethical assessments

7. Determining historical significance

Background on racism

Teaching about racism on page 97

Correlation of the lessons with books in the series

Each lesson can be used with any and all of the books in the Righting Canada's Wrongs series. The *Key topics and references to Righting Canada's Wrongs texts* beginning on page 103 lists the critical thinking questions at the heart of each lesson and specifies, for each book, key topics and factors to consider with relevant page numbers for students to consult.

1.
Reading an image

▶ Critical task

Derive multiple relevant observations and plausible inferences in response to general and specific questions posed about the contents of an assigned image.

▶ Overview

This challenge introduces a three-step approach to analyzing images that students will be encouraged to apply when completing other lessons in this series. As a first step, students formulate a one-sentence summary of the contents of a sample photograph. Next, students undertake a more detailed examination of the image, indicating their answers to each of the 5 Ws questions. Students are then introduced to the difference between what can be directly observed and what might be inferred based on observations. Students revise their answers to the 5 Ws questions in light of this distinction. In the third step, students study the image for more specific information about an assigned topic (for example, architecture of the time, daily life, gender roles). When looking for this information, students undertake a section-by-section reading of the photograph and qualify their conclusions based on the available evidence. Finally, students apply this multi-layered approach to another image (or images) found in one of the books in the Righting Canada's Wrongs series.

Pre-planning

▶ Select images for analysis

Blackline Master #1.1
▶ Sample Image

We suggest introducing the three-step approach to reading images using the sample image found on Blackline Master #1.1 and then applying the approach a second time with different images on a common theme. For the follow-up analysis, you may wish to choose one or more images on a particular topic of interest from a book in the Righting Canada's Wrongs series.

BLACKLINE MASTER #1.1 p. 14 ▶

14 Righting Canada's Wrongs Resource Guide

Session One: Practising Image Analysis

▶ Discuss the value of image analysis

Invite students to speculate about the meaning and the accuracy of the saying: "A picture is worth a thousand words." Ask students to consider, in general terms, what information we can learn by examining historical images (for example, architecture, fashions, modes of transportation, technology use). Explain that in this lesson they will be learning a three-step approach to use when "reading" an image.

▶ Introduce step one: Summary statement

Display the sample image (Blackline Master #1.1) either as a transparency or digital projection. You may also wish to distribute a print copy of the image to each pair of students. Do not reveal the caption ("Canadian troops march on Yonge Street in Toronto during the First World War"). Invite students to formulate a one-sentence response to the question: What is this picture about? Arrange for several students to share their summary sentences and supporting reasons with the rest of the class. Without going into detail, draw attention to any discrepancies in students' answers. For example, is the main action a parade or are troops simply marching through the streets?

▶ Introduce step two: 5 Ws questions

Explain that a useful next step in analyzing an image is to use five questions that reporters ask when trying to explain an event. Write the following 5 Ws questions on the board:

1. Who appears in the image?

2. What is occurring in the image?

3. When does the scene take place?

4. Where does the scene take place?

5. Why are the events in the scene occurring?

Invite students to work with a partner to answer each of these questions and to identify details from the sample image that help them answer each of these questions. Create a chart similar to the following one on the board and ask various students to share their answers.

Questions	Details	Conclusions
Who?	*Men are walking, wearing overalls and hats. They do not appear to be in a hurry.*	*The men are leaving for work that is most likely physical labour.*
What?	*The men are walking through a gate of a barbed wire fence. None of the men are carrying supplies or food.*	*The men are being forced to go to some form of work camp and are likely prisoners.*
When?	*The clothing doesn't look contemporary. There are no signs of modern technology.*	*The lack of electrical wires and clothing suggests this is the early 20th century*
Where?	*There are mountains in the background. The housing appears to be temporary (large tents).*	*This is a rural setting. The mountains suggest it could be somewhere in the Rockies.*
Why?	*There are no prison guards present and no men appear to be attempting to escape.*	*The men appear to be temporarily imprisoned at a remote work camp.*

Invite students to look for other details that might confirm or challenge various conclusions. For example, the lack of prison guards might suggest that the prisoners are not considered a serious threat. This reinforces the conclusion that the men are not likely to attempt escape.

Distinguish observation from inference

Explain that when examining an image, readers often draw conclusions and identify details that are not explicitly observable from the image. Introduce a distinction between what students can actually see in the image (for example, "the men leaving the enclosure are wearing overalls and hats") and the inferences they might draw from these observations (for example, "the men are going to do physical work outdoors"). Point out that the observations provide evidence for the inference. Relabel the headings on the chart as shown below and invite students to confirm whether the details they offered are observations or inferences. As illustrated below, ask students to restate as direct observations any details that included inferences.

Questions	Observations	Inferences
Who?	ORIGINAL: *They are wearing work-style clothes and hats.* CHANGE TO: *The men are walking wearing similar clothing, including jeans, overalls, and hats. They have their hands in their pockets and do not look like they are in a hurry.*	REVISED INFERENCE: *Based on their clothing and body language the men are leaving for work that is most likely physical labor outdoors. They do not appear to be in a hurry to get to work.*

Questions	Observations	Inferences
What?		
When?		
Where?	ORIGINAL: *The housing looks temporary and remote.* CHANGE TO: *The housing in the background appears to be large canvas tents.*	REVISED INFERENCE: *The housing for the men is large tents which is most likely temporary and in a remote area.*
Why?		

Discuss criteria for a thoughtful analysis

Introduce students to the following criteria for the thoughtful analysis of an image:

- *accurate and detailed observations:* the observations that are offered accurately describe the relevant details in the image, including less obvious details

- *plausible and imaginative inferences:* the inferences go beyond the obvious conclusions and are supported by several pieces of evidence found in the image or based on other facts known about the topic

Reveal the published caption for this image ("Ukrainian internees leave their compound for work at Castle Mountain Internment Camp, AB, 1915"). Ask students if they can identify any details from the image or offer other information they know about the time period to support the identification of Ukrainian internees in Alberta during the First World War. (For example, students may narrow down the possible locations by considering what areas of Western Canada were developed at this time and why the internees may have been sent to a remote area instead of an urban prison.)

Introduce step three: Focus questions

Indicate that answers to the 5 Ws questions are useful in explaining the overall contents of any image. Often we want to probe images for specific information about a topic of particular interest (for example, to study clothing fashions, architecture, or daily life). Return students' attention to the sample image. Assign various groups of students a particular focus for a more detailed analysis. These topics might include: quality of life for internees, men's clothing, the setting of internment camps and internment camp construction. Encourage students to look beyond obvious clues, trying to extract as much information as possible from the image.

Provide guidance for step three

Before students begin to study the sample image to learn about their assigned topic, offer these suggestions to guide their reading of the picture:

What do I already know about the topic? Take a minute to make a list of information they already have about their assigned topic and time period.

What I can tell about the topic from a sector-by-sector analysis? Rather than randomly looking at the picture, organize a close reading of the image using one of these methods:

- **Rows:** Divide the image into three horizontal rows and analyze the foreground, middle, and background.

- **Panels:** Divide the image into three vertical rows and analyze the left panel, middle panel, and right panel.

- **Quadrants:** Divide the image into four quadrants and look closely at each section. Explain that the composition of the image often suggests which way of segmenting the image may be more useful: for example, viewing the image in panels works when there are sections of relevant details on the sides of the image (as is the case if exploring setting or environment in the sample image); a complicated picture that has evenly distributed relevant detail may be best viewed in four quadrants (the bottom two quadrants are most useful if exploring the men's clothing); outside landscape images or images with depth of view often are best approached in rows (perhaps, if exploring the remoteness of the camps or the construction of internment housing).

How plausible are my conclusions? Encourage students to assess the plausibility of each of their inferences in light of corroborating details in the image or in other images or sources. If students know little about the topic and are faced with limited or inconclusive detail in the image, encourage them to be tentative in stating their inferences. Suggest that they qualify tentative conclusions by using terms such as "may be," "possibly," and "perhaps."

Direct students' investigations

Arrange for students to work in pairs or groups of three to review what they already know about their assigned topic; to study the image section-by-section looking for relevant details and drawing inferences about the topic; and finally to summarize and qualify any conclusions. After each team has "read" the sample image, arrange for other teams with the same topic to share their findings with each other. Finally, ask a few students to share what they have learned about their assigned topic with the entire class.

Session Two: Historical Image Analysis

Introduce a new analysis

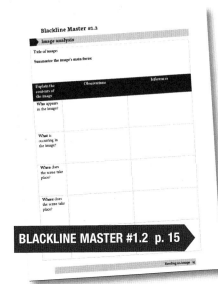

BLACKLINE MASTER #1.2 p. 15

Invite students to use the three-step analysis to examine one or more images from the Righting Canada's Wrongs series. Begin by distributing both pages of *Image analysis* (Blackline Master #1.2) to each student. Review the three-step approach:

• summarize the image's main focus in a sentence;

• explain the contents of the image using the 5 Ws questions to make observations and draw inferences;

• conduct an in-depth reading of the image on a particular topic by reviewing prior knowledge, making relevant observations and drawing inferences based on a section-by-section analysis, and summarizing and qualifying all relevant conclusions.

Provide students with a specific topic (or different topics) to consider as they make observations and draw inferences. Ask students individually or in groups to analyze the assigned photographs on a common theme and to record their findings at each step of the analysis on Blackline Master #1.2.

Share findings

Once students have completed their analyses, arrange for them to share their findings with other students investigating the same topic. Finally, invite a few students to share what they have learned about their assigned topic with the entire class. Discuss the challenges that students face as they try to "read" images, and the usefulness of the approach they have just applied.

Assess the image analysis

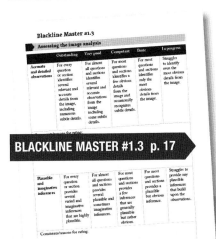

BLACKLINE MASTER #1.3 p. 17

Assess students' ability to make accurate and detailed observations and to draw plausible and imaginative conclusions about an image as recorded on Blackline Master #1.2, using the rubric found on *Assessing the image analysis* (Blackline Master #1.3).

Prepare for future applications

Suggest to students that it may be useful for them to complete Blackline Master #1.2 in writing for a few of the images they will analyze. However, once they become familiar with the approach, they may spend less time on the first two steps, perhaps completing them orally. In addition, while students are encouraged to undertake a section-by-section analysis of any image, they may prefer to record all their observations and inferences, even those from several images, in a single two-column chart.

Blackline Master #1.1

Image © Glenbow Archives

Blackline Master #1.2

Title of image:

Summarize the image's main focus:

Explain the contents of the image	Observations	Inferences
Who appears in the image?		
What is occurring in the image?		
When does the scene take place?		
Where does the scene take place?		
Why are the events in the scene occurring?		

Identify a topic to explore in-depth:

Review what you already know about this topic:

What can I learn about the topic in each section of the image?	Observations	Inferences
Check applicable section: Foreground Left panel Top left		
Check applicable section: Middleground Middle panel Bottom left		
Check applicable section: Background Right panel Top right		
Bottom right (if applicable)		

Summarize and qualify conclusions about the topic:

Blackline Master #1.3

Assessing the image analysis

	Outstanding	Very good	Competent	Basic	In progress
Accurate and detailed observations	For every question or section identifies several relevant and accurate details from the image, including numerous subtle details.	For almost all questions and sections identifies several relevant and accurate observations from the image including some subtle details.	For most questions and sections identifies a few obvious details from the image and occasionally recognizes subtle details.	For most questions and sections identifies only the most obvious details from the image.	Struggles to identify even the most obvious details from the image.
Comments/reasons for rating:					
Plausible and imaginative inferences	For every question or section provides several varied and imaginative inferences that are highly plausible.	For almost all questions and sections provides several plausible and sometimes imaginative inferences.	For most questions and sections provides a few inferences that are generally plausible but rather obvious.	For most questions and sections provides a plausible but obvious inference.	Struggles to provide any plausible inferences that build upon the observations.
Comments/reasons for rating:					

2.
Adopting historical perspectives

Critical tasks

A. Draw historically plausible conclusions about the experiences and attitudes of a featured group regarding some aspect of a historical injustice.

B. Write a letter from the point of view of a teenage member of the group explaining the specified situation or event.

Overview

In this two-part critical challenge, students learn to take on the historical perspective of a group by analyzing primary and secondary sources from the Righting Canada's Wrongs series. Students are introduced to the idea of historical perspective-taking using the example of postal services in the nineteenth century. They consider the difference between presentism and historical perspective-taking and learn about three strategies to help in adopting a historical perspective. Students are then asked to examine textual and visual sources to learn about an assigned group's perspective on some aspect of a specified historical injustice. They record relevant details from the sources, draw possible conclusions, and summarize what they have learned about the group's experiences and reactions. Drawing upon these findings, students write a letter from the point of view of a teenager at the time, explaining the specified situation.

Pre-planning

Select the featured event

Prior to introducing the topic to students, determine which injustice (or injustices) featured in the Righting Canada's Wrongs series you wish to explore. Consult the *Key topics and references to Righting Canada's Wrongs texts* (page 103) for specific aspects of the injustice(s) that students are to examine (for example, life before the featured incident, the hardships endured because of the injustice, the redress provided to people who suffered the injustice). Consider assigning different aspects of the injustice to various students individually or in pairs. Make note of the relevant pages in the publication(s) that students might consult when taking on the historical perspective.

Session One: Shifting Perspectives

Present the sample scenario

Present students with the following scenario to illustrate the challenges of trying to understand the mindset of people living in a different time.

> *In 1858 people living in the British colony on Vancouver Island waited four to five months to receive a response to a letter sent from Victoria, BC, to London, England. This meant that important news from friends and family, or advice and instructions from superiors, took almost half a year to arrive.*

Invite students to speculate briefly with a partner on what it might have been like for people in the past to wait this length of time before receiving return correspondence from the home country.

Discuss students' initial responses

Many students may react to the sample scenario from a modern-day perspective influenced by their experiences in living at a time of instantaneous access to news from friends and family via Twitter, Facebook, cell phones, Skype, and email. When responding with a modern-day lens, students may suggest that the colonists:

- were probably frustrated to have to wait so long to hear news from their homeland.

- might think that this method of communication was inefficient and needed to be improved.

- would have felt very isolated because it took so long to receive correspondence or news from England.

Contrast historical perspective with presentism

Explain that adopting a historical perspective is not a matter of thinking of how students personally would have felt in a particular historical situation, but how people at the time would likely have felt. One of the primary obstacles to historical perspective-taking is presentism, the tendency to use present-day values, beliefs, and experiences to interpret the past. When studying history, students often use modern-day lenses that distort the past and what it meant for the people living at the time. Invite students to think back to their initial responses to postal services in 1858. Which of their comments were indicative of a presentist perspective? Which were sensitive to a historical perspective?

Introduce strategies for historical perspective-taking

In trying to nurture historical perspective-taking, encourage students to consider three strategies:

- Anticipate different beliefs and values: Don't presume that historical attitudes, values, and beliefs are identical to those that people currently hold.

- Expect different conditions: Sensitively imagine the realities of the time to understand what would seem unfamiliar (or very familiar) now, but would be commonplace (or foreign) back then.

- Attend to different meanings: Be attentive to the fact that words and gestures may not have had the same meanings or connotations in the past as they do now.

Reconsider initial reactions

Illustrate the application of these strategies by presenting additional information about mail service at the time:

Although mail service between Victoria and London in 1858 was still measured in months, it had improved greatly in the preceding decade. The turnaround time had been reduced almost by half, thanks to improvements in transportation, especially in the novel application of steam power to ocean transport.

Invite students to reconsider the colonists' likely beliefs, conditions, and meanings associated with a four- to five-month wait to receive a response to a letter (down from almost a year-long wait). Individually or in groups, ask students to share their responses. Possible responses may include:

Beliefs
- People might feel pleased to receive such a quick (relatively-speaking) response.

- People might feel that the speed of communication is much improved compared to a decade earlier.

- People might feel less isolated and more connected to people in England than they had felt previously.

Conditions
- There was very limited communication with the outside world.

- People would not have access to any digital technologies.

Meanings
- Instead of viewing a letter as "snail mail," old-fashioned and slow, people may have looked upon mail as exciting news and as a marvel of "modern" technology.

Invite students to share one idea that has changed from their initial thoughts about the reactions of people in the mid-nineteenth century towards the speed of the postal service.

View video on historical perspective-taking

OPTIONAL: Invite students to watch the short Take 2 video on *Historical perspective* prepared by The Critical Thinking Consortium. Discuss the examples and the factors explained in this video.
 http://tinyurl.com/rcwthinkingabouthistory

Introduce the featured injustice

Inform students that they will now explore an injustice committed against a featured group as seen from the perspective of people living at the time. They will examine historical evidence from various primary and secondary sources to draw conclusions about the beliefs, conditions, and meanings associated with some aspect of the injustice. Assign students individually or in groups to one of the injustices featured in the Righting Canada's Wrongs series.

Provide historical context

Ensure that students understand the historical context for the assigned injustice(s) by inviting them to read and discuss the introductory pages of the relevant book in the Righting Canada's Wrongs series. Alternatively, ask students to share information they already know about the injustice.

Session Two: Historical Perspective-Taking

Introduce the first critical task

BLACKLINE MASTER #2.1 p. 26

Inform students that their first task is to look for clues from relevant sources in the Righting Canada's Wrongs series about the historical perspective of a featured group on an aspect of the historical injustice. Identify the specific aspect of the injustice you wish each student to explore. Draw students' attention to the relevant page numbers in the Righting Canada's Wrongs series for their assigned event or situation as indicated in the *Key topics and references to Righting Canada's Wrongs texts* (page 103). Distribute copies of *Identifying historical perspectives* (Blackline Master #2.1) to students individually or in pairs. Explain to students that they can use this sheet to record information and draw conclusions about the likely experiences and reactions of a featured group to the assigned situation or event.

Discuss criteria for historical perspective-taking

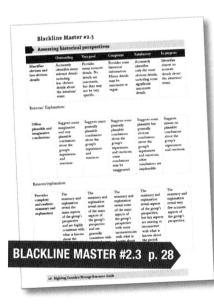

BLACKLINE MASTER #2.3 p. 28

Distribute a copy of the rubric *Assessing historical perspectives* (Blackline Master #2.3) and discuss the following criteria:

• Identifies many relevant details, including less obvious details that indicate the beliefs, conditions, and meanings of the time.

• Offers plausible and imaginative conclusions that are consistent with one or more clues in the historical documents about the group's experiences and reactions in connection with the featured situation or event.

• Provides a thoughtful summary of their conclusions with reasons why their findings are grounded in historical facts and not a result of a presentist perspective.

Direct students' analyses

Before students begin, you may wish to model completion of Blackline Master #2.1 using a sample image (or perhaps a document). If students have had little experience with image analysis, introduce the strategies described in the lesson plan *Reading an image* (beginning on page 7). When you are ready to start, introduce a sample text or image to analyze. Direct students to look for obvious and less obvious clues about the beliefs, conditions, and meanings associated with the assigned situation or event. Record ideas in the first column of Blackline Master #2.1. Be sure that the details are relevant to the group's perspective. Instruct students to record their tentative conclusions about the group's experiences and reactions in the second column. When students are not certain about their conclusions, encourage them to qualify their statements with words such as "maybe," "might," or "perhaps." Direct students to examine a few other documents and images found on the assigned pages.

Share and review partial work

BLACKLINE MASTER #2.2 p. 27

When students have recorded details and possible conclusions for a few documents and images, arrange for them to exchange their work with another student. Encourage students to use *Peer assessment of perspective-taking* (Blackline Master #2.2) to review each other's work. Encourage students to find details from each other's work that offer evidence of how well they did, to offer an overall assessment of the work, and to make helpful suggestions. Encourage students to consider the feedback they received when continuing with their analysis of the remaining assigned documents and images. After students have recorded details and possible conclusions from all of the assigned pages, direct them to summarize their findings on the bottom of Blackline Master #2.1 and to explain how and why this perspective differs from the views that people living today might hold. In other words, direct students to explain why their portrayal isn't the result of a presentist perspective.

Assess the completed analyses

When students have finished their analyses of the assigned pages, assess their completed copies of Blackline Master #2.1 using the rubric *Assessing historical perspectives* (Blackline Master #2.3). Based on feedback from your assessment, encourage students to locate additional information about the event or to review some of the previously analyzed sources.

Session Three: Letters From the Past

Introduce the historically realistic letter

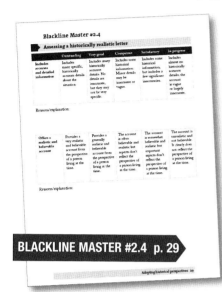

BLACKLINE MASTER #2.4 p. 29

Inform students that their next task is to assume the role of a teenager from their assigned group and write a historically realistic letter to a relative, a newspaper editor, a government official, or other historical person explaining the experiences and reactions associated with the featured situation or event. Encourage students to portray the historical perspective of a young person writing at the time. You may want to share copies of the rubric found on *Assessing a historically realistic letter* (Blackline Master #2.4) with students. Explain the two criteria for the assignment:

- offer accurate and detailed information about the situation they are explaining;

- provide a realistic and believable account written from the perspective of a young person living at the time.

Discuss the lessons learned

When students have completed drafts of their letters, arrange for them to share with other students of the same featured group; or, if you have chosen to study multiple groups, with members of different groups. Reflect as a class on the experiences and attitudes of the various historical groups, and the difficulties of adopting a historical perspective. In light of what they have just learned, encourage students to revise their letters prior to submitting them for assessment.

Assess the letters

Assess students' revised letters using the rubric found on *Assessing a historically realistic letter* (Blackline Master #2.4).

Blackline Master #2.1

Featured group:
Situation or event:

Details about the beliefs, conditions, and meanings associated with the situation or event	Possible conclusions about the group's experiences and attitudes

Summary of the group's experiences and attitudes:

Differences from a present-day perspective:

Blackline Master #2.2

Identifies many relevant details including less obvious details about historical beliefs, conditions, and meanings associated with the assigned situation or event

/_____/_____/_____/_____/
Excellent   Not yet

Evidence for the rating	Suggestions for improvement

Offers plausible and imaginative conclusions about the historical experiences and reactions

/_____/_____/_____/_____/
Excellent   Not yet

Evidence for the rating	Suggestions for improvement

Blackline Master #2.3

Assessing historical perspectives

	Outstanding	Very good	Competent	Satisfactory	In progress
Identifies obvious and less obvious details	Accurately identifies many relevant details including less obvious details about the situation/event.	Provides many accurate details. No details are inaccurate, but they may not be very specific.	Provides some historical information. Minor details may be inaccurate or vague.	Accurately identifies only the most obvious details, including some significant inaccurate details.	Identifies almost no accurate details about the situation/event.

Reasons/ Explanation:

Offers plausible and imaginative conclusions	Suggests many imaginative and very plausible conclusions about the group's experiences and reactions.	Suggests many generally plausible conclusions about the group's experiences and reactions	Suggests some generally plausible conclusions about the group's experiences and reactions; some conclusions may be exaggerated.	Suggests some plausible but generally obvious conclusions about the group's experiences and reactions; other conclusions are implausible.	Suggests almost no plausible conclusions about the group's experiences and reactions.

Reasons/explanation:

Provides complete and realistic summary and explanation	The summary and explanation reveal the main aspects of the group's perspective and are highly consistent with what is known about the period.	The summary and explanation reveal most of the main aspects of the group's perspective and are generally consistent with what is known about the period.	The summary and explanation reveal some of the main aspects of the group's perspective with some inconsistencies with what is known about the period.	The summary and explanation reveal aspects of the group's perspective, but key aspects are missing or inconsistent with what is known about the period.	The summary and explanation reveal very few accurate aspects of the group's perspective.

Reasons/explanation:

Blackline Master #2.4

Assessing a historically realistic letter

	Outstanding	Very good	Competent	Satisfactory	In progress
Includes accurate and detailed information	Includes many specific, historically accurate details about the situation.	Includes many historically accurate details. No details are inaccurate, but they may not be very specific.	Includes some historical information. Minor details may be inaccurate or vague.	Includes some historical information, but includes a few significant inaccuracies.	Includes almost no historically accurate details; the account is vague or largely inaccurate.

Reasons/explanation:

Offers a realistic and believable account	Provides a very realistic and believable account from the perspective of a person living at the time.	Provides a generally realistic and believable account from the perspective of a person living at the time.	The account is often believable and realistic but aspects don't reflect the perspective of a person living at the time.	The account is somewhat believable and realistic but important aspects don't reflect the perspective of a person living at the time.	The account is unrealistic and not believable. It clearly does not reflect the perspective of a person living at the time.

Reasons/explanation:

3.
Tracking continuity and change

▶ Critical tasks

A. Identify the similarities and differences between the experiences of two groups or a single group over two time periods.

B. Identify the most important similarity and difference between the compared groups or time periods.

▶ Overview

In this two-part challenge, students investigate continuity and change between groups or time periods featured in the Righting Canada's Wrongs series. Students begin by tracking similarities and differences at two comparison points in their own lives: primary school and secondary school. After discussing criteria for assessing the relative importance, students identify the most important similarity and most important difference between two periods in their lives. Students then investigate the similarities and differences in the experiences of featured groups using primary and secondary sources found in the Righting Canada's Wrongs series. Finally, students determine the most important similarities and differences between the featured groups or time periods.

Pre-planning

▶ Select the featured event

Prior to introducing the topic to students, determine which groups or time periods featured in the Righting Canada's Wrongs series you wish to explore. Consult the *Key topics and references to Righting Canada's Wrongs texts* (page 103) for specific comparisons that students might explore (for example, life before and after the unjust treatment, the nature and impact of sanctioned injustices for different groups). Consider comparing the experiences of featured groups found in different books in the Righting Canada's Wrongs series. Make note of the relevant pages in the publication(s) that students might consult when tracking continuity and change.

Session One: Understanding Continuity and Change

▶ Introduce continuity and change

Introduce the concepts of continuity and change by indicating that you will soon ask students to think of aspects of their lives that have remained the same from when they were in primary school and those that have changed since then. As a class, brainstorm categories of life experiences to compare (e.g., school life, home life, relationships). Explain that you will want students to think of examples of similarities and differences within each of these categories. To illustrate what you will soon require of them, suggest several actual or hypothetical examples from your own life experiences. Record your responses in a chart such as the one shown below.

▶ Sample response

Comparing my life at age six and now

Similarities	Differences
Relationships	
Many of my closest relationships are with the same groups of people: my parents, siblings, my school friends.	*I have more friends now.* *People who were my best friends then are no longer my closest friends.*
School life	
Regular school hours are very similar now to when I was six. Classes began around 9 am and finished around 3 pm. *The basic structure of a classroom has changed very little. There are around thirty students and one teacher. There are tables and chairs and boards for teachers to instruct on.*	*The level of difficulty of lesson materials has changed significantly since primary school.* *In high school, students learn different subjects in different rooms with different teachers and classmates.*
Home life	
Home remains the place where the majority of my meals are eaten and leisure time is spent. *A similar daily routine and schedule is kept; morning routine, eating, and sleeping patterns.*	*I now have complete responsibility over my eating, sleeping, and leisure schedule at home.* *Entertainment and food preparation technologies have advanced significantly.*

Explore continuity and change in their own lives

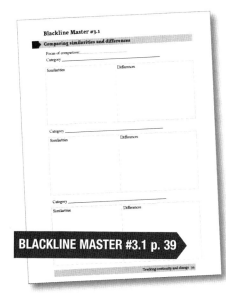

BLACKLINE MASTER #3.1 p. 39

Ask students to complete *Comparing similarities and differences* (Blackline Master #3.1) individually or in groups. Students are to record the agreed-upon categories and list as many similarities and differences in each category as they can. After completing this activity, invite students to share their observations in small groups or with the entire class. Draw out from the discussion that in all aspects of their lives, some things are changing, while other things stay the same.

Introduce criteria for judging importance

Invite students to consider whether all of the similarities and differences between the two time periods are equally important. For example, is moving to a new city or country a bigger change in one's life than modifications in hairstyles over the years? Introduce the following criteria for determining whether some similarities and differences are more important than others.

Criteria for an important change:

• Substantial effect (a dramatic difference in the way the thing functions).

• Relatively permanent (not easily reversible).

• Widespread (affects a wide breadth of things and has a wide scope of impact).

Criteria for an important continuity:

• Makes little if any difference in what happens.

• Involves a key aspect of people's lives, not a trivial similarity.

• Widespread constancy across a breadth of things—reaches many people, involves frequent events.

Judge important aspects in students' lives

BLACKLINE MASTER #3.2 p. 40

Distribute a copy of *Judging important differences and similarities* (Blackline Master #3.2) to students individually or in pairs. Explain that they are to identify three significant differences and three significant similarities in their lives between primary school and secondary school. They should then provide evidence related to the criteria discussed above for each aspect. Finally, ask students to use these criteria to judge the most important difference and the most important similarity. After completing this activity, invite students to share their conclusions in small groups or with the entire class.

Self-assess the analysis of continuity and change

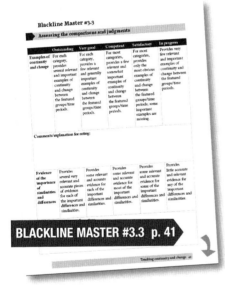

BLACKLINE MASTER #3.3 p. 41

Distribute a copy of the rubric found on *Assessing the comparisons and judgments* (Blackline Master #3.3). Ask each student or pair of students to review the completed copy of Blackline Masters #3.1 and #3.2 in light of the criteria described in the rubric. Review any issues that students may not have understood.

View video on historical continuity and change

OPTIONAL: Invite students to watch the short Take 2 video on *Continuity and change* prepared by The Critical Thinking Consortium. Discuss the examples and the factors explained in the video.

 http://tinyurl.com/rcwthinkingabouthistory

Session Two: Investigating Continuity and Change

Introduce the featured historical group(s)

Inform students that they will consider the changes and constants related to the experiences of one or more groups of people who suffered an injustice committed by a government. First, they will examine various primary and secondary sources to determine similarities and differences between groups or time periods, and then select the most important similarities and differences. Assign students individually or in groups to compare groups or time periods featured in Righting Canada's Wrongs.

Provide historical context

Ensure that students understand the historical context for the assigned groups or time periods by inviting them to read and discuss the introductory pages of the relevant book(s) in the Righting Canada's Wrongs series. Alternatively, ask students to share information they already know about the topic.

Introduce the first critical task

Inform students that their first task is to look for clues from relevant sources in the Righting Canada's Wrongs series about similarities and differences in social, political, and economic experiences of featured groups or between time periods. Draw students' attention to the relevant page numbers in the Righting Canada's Wrongs series and ask them to select a group and time period to compare.

Distribute copies of *Comparing similarities and differences* (Blackline Master #3.1) to students individually or in pairs to record similarities and differences between the featured groups or time periods.

Explain the need to draw inferences

Before students begin making observations and inferences from the sources, discuss the following criteria:

Effective observations

- include both obvious and less obvious features;

- are relevant to the experiences of featured groups;

- accurately reflect the various categories of experience.

Thoughtful inferences

- are plausible;

- are supported by evidence;

- provide insight into the situation.

Offer an example connected to a featured group to illustrate how some sources enable readers to draw explicit or obvious inferences about that group's experiences and conditions. Find another example, where viewers must read "between the lines" or draw implicit inferences about the group's circumstances.

▶ Introduce three categories of experiences

Explain to students that it is helpful to organize their comparisons of historical experiences into the following categories:

Political: Relating or concerned with their rights and freedoms as citizens and the involvement or influence of government and the legal system

Social: Relating to the quality of the interaction with others and the ability to take part in daily events involving others.

Economic: Relating to their ability and conditions for work and to earn and enjoy a livelihood

As a class, work through two paired sample sources to demonstrate how to make observations and draw inferences about similarities and differences in social, political, and economic experiences. You may choose to compare groups using different sources (e.g. *Righting Canada's Wrongs: Japanese Canadian Internment in the Second World War* and *Righting Canada's Wrongs: Italian Canadian Internment in the Second World War*) or decide to compare the same group at two different time periods.

Category: <u>Economic experiences</u>

Similarities	Differences
In both time periods, Japanese and Chinese Canadians worked in labour-intensive, physically demanding, and low-paying industries.	The locations of work are different. Large numbers of Chinese Canadians engaged in labour-intensive railway work, while many Japanese Canadians worked on fishing boats or in the fish canneries and would likely have lived on the coast in company dwellings.

▶ Complete the identification of similarities and differences

Direct students to study the assigned pages looking for evidence of social, political, and economic similarities and differences. When students have gathered and recorded this information on Blackline Master #3.1, arrange for them to share their findings with the rest of the class. Discuss with students the ongoing presence of continuity and change. Invite students to identify how certain experiences changed in some ways and were similar in other ways.

Session Three: Judging Importance

► Judge important similarities and differences

Explain to students that their next task is to select the most important similarity and difference from among the changes and continuities they have identified between the two time periods or groups. Remind students of the criteria for important continuity and change:

Important difference: has a substantial effect, is relatively permanent, is widespread;

Important similarity: little if any change over time, focuses on a key aspect of people's lives, is not a trivial similarity, is widespread or frequently experienced.

Distribute a copy of *Judging important differences and similarities* (Blackline Master #3.2) to each student. Explain to students that they must identify three important changes listed on Blackline Master #3.1, and then decide which of these is the most important change. They should then repeat the process for the most important continuity. Remind students to look for evidence of importance in the designated primary and secondary sources from the Righting Canada's Wrongs series.

► Discuss the lessons learned

Invite students to share their choices of most important similarity and difference and the reasons for these judgments with the rest of the class. Discuss whether students were surprised by certain findings.

► Evaluate students' conclusions

Assess each student's identification of examples of similarities and differences and their justification for the most important similarity and difference using the rubric found on *Assessing the comparisons and judgments* (Blackline Master #3.3).

Blackline Master #3.1

Comparing similarities and differences

Focus of comparison:_____

Category _____

Similarities	Differences

Category _____

Similarities	Differences

Category _____

Similarities	Differences

Blackline Master #3.2

Describe three differences	Evidence of important change Summarize what is known about the depth of its effect, its permanence, and how widespread its impact was

Explanation for the most important difference:

Describe three similarities	Evidence of important continuity Summarize what is known about its lack of effect, its key role in people's lives, and how widespread it was

Explanation for the most important similarity:

Blackline Master #3.3

► **Assessing the comparisons and judgments**

	Outstanding	Very good	Competent	Satisfactory	In progress
Examples of continuity and change	For each category, provides several relevant and important examples of continuity and change between the featured groups/time periods.	For each category, provides a few relevant and generally important examples of continuity and change between the featured groups/time periods.	For most categories, provides a few relevant and somewhat important examples of continuity and change between the featured groups/time periods.	For most categories, provides only the most obvious examples of continuity and change between the featured groups/time periods; some important examples are missing.	Provides very few relevant and important examples of continuity and change between the featured groups/time periods.
Comments/explanation for rating:					
Evidence of the importance of similarities and differences	Provides several very relevant and accurate pieces of evidence for each of the important differences and similarities.	Provides some relevant and accurate evidence for each of the important differences and similarities.	Provides some relevant and accurate evidence for most of the important differences and similarities.	Provides some relevant and accurate evidence for some of the important differences and similarities.	Provides little accurate and relevant evidence for any of the important differences and similarities.
Comments/explanation for rating:					

Reasons for the most important similarity and difference	Offers several specific and very convincing reasons for the selected most important similarity and most important difference.	Offers several specific and somewhat convincing reasons for the selected most important similarity and most important difference.	Offers a few convincing, though vague, reasons for the selected most important similarity and most important difference.	Offers a few relevant reasons for the selected most important similarity and most important difference, but some of the most convincing reasons are omitted or vaguely explained.	Offers very vague or unconvincing reasons for both the selected most important similarity and most important difference.

Comments/explanation for rating:

4.
Examining historical causation

Critical task

A. Identify the various underlying and immediate causes of a particular event.

B. Determine the three most important contributing factors to the event.

Overview

In this challenge, students learn to identify the range of underlying and immediate causes leading to a historical event featured in the Righting Canada's Wrongs series. Students are first introduced to the concept of causation by identifying various factors that caused a car accident. They learn to distinguish between underlying and immediate causes by grouping the causes for the car accident. Students then consider the criteria for assessing the importance of causes. Next, students examine a variety of primary and secondary sources from the Righting Canada's Wrongs series to gather information about the contributing role of various factors to an assigned event. They identify the many underlying or immediate causal factors that contributed to the event and gather evidence about their impact. Finally, students determine the three most important contributing factors to the event.

Pre-planning

Select the featured event

Prior to introducing the topic to students, determine which injustice (or injustices) featured in the Righting Canada's Wrongs series you wish to explore. Consult the *Key topics and references to Righting Canada's Wrongs texts* (page 103) for the specific event(s) that students are to analyze for their causal factors (for example, why the injustice occurred, or what factors contributed to a decision to provide redress to people who suffered the injustice). Consider assigning different events to various students individually or in pairs. Make note of the relevant pages in the publication(s) that students might consult when identifying the causes of their assigned event.

Session One: What Caused the Accident?

Introduce the concept of causation

Explain to students that when historians study the past, they do more than simply recount a sequence of events. They strive to explain why events happened the way they did. Historians often ask questions such as, "What caused the First World War?" or "Did increased use of birth control affect women's status in society?" In asking these questions, historians are not looking for a single factor that brought about the event; rather they are looking to identify the many factors, including broad social, political, and economic conditions, that contributed to its occurrence.

Recognize various causal factors

Invite students to identify a range of causes by considering a series of events leading to a fictional car accident. Distribute *Identifying the causes of the accident* (Blackline Master #4.1) to each pair of students and ask them to identify all the possible causes that they can locate in the account of the accident. Invite students to share their lists of contributing factors with the rest of the class.

Introduce underlying and immediate causes

Explain to students that the difficulty in determining causation is that direct causes seldom act on their own as catalysts for change. Often underlying causes and broader trends create the conditions that trigger significant change. For example, the start of the First World War is often attributed to the assassination of Archduke Franz Ferdinand. However, a war does not break out each time a leader is killed. A broader set of circumstances existed that enable the killing of a leader to trigger a global conflict. These broader factors and circumstances—called underlying causes—are often distinguished from immediate causes:

> **immediate causes:** the direct and often the most obvious and easily identified factors. They typically occur just prior to the event in question. Removal of immediate causes may not have prevented the occurrence of the event, as there are often other significant factors contributing to the event.

underlying causes: the broader and usually less obvious and more difficult to identify conditions. They are often a broader underlying factor, practice, or belief and not tied to a single event. Removal of an underlying cause may help prevent the event from occurring.

Suggest the following metaphor to distinguish immediate and underlying causes. Immediate causes are igniters of events. They are the flints, matches, or lighters that start a fire. However, if a match, flint, or lighter has no kindling, dry grass, or wood to burn, it will quickly fizzle out and will not cause the fire to start. The kindling, dry grass, and wood represent the underlying causes that are often the foundational causes of an event, and the causes that will propel an event forward. Underlying causes merit attention because they create the circumstances for historical change.

Recognizing immediate and underlying causes

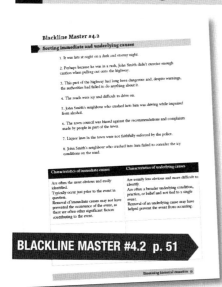

BLACKLINE MASTER #4.2 p. 51

Distribute copies of *Sorting immediate and underlying causes* (Blackline Master #4.2) to each pair of students. It lists eight of the contributing factors to the previously discussed car accident. Invite students to classify the causes into immediate and underlying. Provide an example of an immediate cause (e.g., the victim had run out of cigarettes) and a broader underlying cause (e.g., lax law enforcement of drunk drivers). After completing the task, invite students to discuss their conclusions. Below are samples of answers that students might offer.

Immediate causes	Underlying causes
It was late in the evening on a dark and stormy night.	*This part of the highway had long been dangerous and, despite warnings, the authorities had failed to do anything about it.*
Perhaps because he was in a rush, John Smith didn't exercise enough caution when pulling out onto the highway.	*The town council was biased against recommendations and complaints made by people in this part of the town.*
The roads were icy and difficult to drive on.	*Liquor laws in the town were not faithfully enforced by the police.*
John Smith's neighbour who crashed into him was driving while impaired from alcohol.	
John Smith's neighbour who crashed into him failed to consider the icy conditions on the road.	

Assess the relative importance of causes

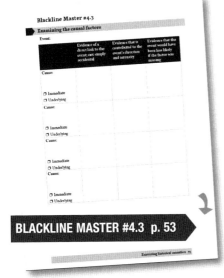

BLACKLINE MASTER #4.3 p. 53

Ask students to consider whether all the causes are equally important—whether some factors are more instrumental than others in bringing about and shaping the event. Distribute copies of *Examining the causal factors* (Blackline Master #4.3) to each pair of students. Direct students to consider three criteria for determining the importance of causes:

- The cause was a directly linked factor to the event occurring and not simply an accidental occurrence (i.e., it gave rise to causes that were catalysts for the event).

- The factor was an important contributor to the direction and intensity of the event (e.g., a careful driver going slowly might still have hit Smith's car but not necessarily killed him).

- The event would be much less likely to have occurred if the cause was not present (e.g., Smith may not have been killed that night, but speeding cars may eventually have claimed his life if the highway was dangerous).

Ask students to record reasons for each identified cause related to these three criteria. Once they have done this, invite students to judge the three most important causes that led to the accident. Arrange for students to share their priority causes and supporting reasons. As a class, attempt to reach consensus on the most important causes.

Self-assess the examination of causal factors

BLACKLINE MASTER #4.4 p. 55

Distribute a copy of the rubric found on *Assessing the causal analysis* (Blackline Master #4.4). Ask each pair of students to review their completed copies of Blackline Master #4.3 in light of the class discussion and the criteria in the assessment rubric. Review any issues that students may not have understood.

View video on historical cause and consequence

OPTIONAL: Invite students to watch the short Take 2 video on *Cause and consequence* prepared by The Critical Thinking Consortium. Discuss the examples and the factors explained in this video.

 http://tinyurl.com/rcwthinkingabouthistory

Session Two: Determining Causal Factors

▶ Consider the causes of a historical injustice

Inform students that they will consider the contributing factors to an event associated with an injustice committed by the government against a particular group. This will entail examination of historical evidence from a variety of primary and secondary sources to determine possible causes, and then to identify those that seem most important. Assign students individually or in groups to an event associated with one of the injustices featured in the Righting Canada's Wrongs series.

▶ Provide historical context

Ensure that students understand the historical context for the assigned event by inviting them to read appropriate pages in the Righting Canada's Wrongs series that introduce the event or by reviewing what they already know about it.

▶ Research the causal factors

Encourage students to consult the pages in the Righting Canada's Wrongs series associated with their assigned event. Distribute copies of *Examining the causal factors* (Blackline Master #4.3). Ask students to identify and list the causes of the event, classify those causes into immediate and underlying causes, and collect the following evidence on each causal factor:

- how it is directly linked to the event;

- how it contributed to the direction and intensity of the event;

- why the event would be less likely to have occurred if the cause was not present.

When students have completed their research, invite them to determine the three most important causes. Ask students to provide reasons for the special importance of the three selected causes.

▶ Share conclusions

When finished, invite students to share with the rest of the class their list of identified causes, indicating the three most important causes and their justifications.

Assess the causal analysis

Assess each student's completed version of Blackline Master #4.3 using the criteria in the assessment rubric found on Blackline Master #4.4.

Blackline Master #4.1

Identifying the causes of the accident

Just before midnight one dark and stormy night, a man called John Smith, an engine mechanic, was sitting in an isolated cabin in the woods. As he reached for a cigarette, he noticed he had only one left. Glancing at his watch, he realized he had just enough time to hop in his car and drive to the gas station down the road to buy cigarettes before it closed. As his car pulled out of his lane and onto the highway, it was hit by his neighbour, who, returning from a long night of drinking, was unable to stop his car soon enough on the icy road. Smith was killed instantly. Later, as the townspeople were discussing the sad event, they shook their heads and said, "We always knew that smoking would kill Smith." It is worth noting that local officials had long been warned of the dangers of that part of the highway, especially in winter, and yet they seemed uninterested in doing anything about it—apparently because the residents of that part of the town did not have any influence with local authorities. Others wondered whether the neighbour who smashed into Smith would have been as drunk as he was if the impaired driving laws had been more faithfully enforced in the town.[1]

List the contributing factors to the accident:

---

1   Taken from *Heaven & Hell on Earth: The Massacre of the "Black" Donnellys*, part of the Great Unsolved Mysteries in Canadian History series: www.canadianmysteries.ca

Blackline Master #4.2

Sorting immediate and underlying causes

1. It was late at night on a dark and stormy night.

2. Perhaps because he was in a rush, John Smith didn't exercise enough caution when pulling out onto the highway.

3. This part of the highway had long been dangerous and, despite warnings, the authorities had failed to do anything about it.

4. The roads were icy and difficult to drive on.

5. John Smith's neighbour who crashed into him was driving while impaired from alcohol.

6. The town council was biased against the recommendations and complaints made by people in part of the town.

7. Liquor laws in the town were not faithfully enforced by the police.

8. John Smith's neighbour who crashed into him failed to consider the icy conditions on the road.

Characteristics of immediate causes	Characteristics of underlying causes
Are often the most obvious and easily identified. Typically occur just prior to the event in question. Removal of immediate causes may not have prevented the occurrence of the event, as there are often other significant factors contributing to the event.	Are usually less obvious and more difficult to identify. Are often a broader underlying condition, practice, or belief and not tied to a single event. Removal of an underlying cause may have helped prevent the event from occurring.

Characteristics of immediate causes	Characteristics of underlying causes

Blackline Master #4.3

Examining the causal factors

Event:

	Evidence of a direct link to the event; not simply accidental	Evidence that it contributed to the event's direction and intensity	Evidence that the event would have been less likely if the factor was missing
Cause: ❐ Immediate ❐ Underlying			
Cause: ❐ Immediate ❐ Underlying			
Cause: ❐ Immediate ❐ Underlying			
Cause: ❐ Immediate ❐ Underlying			

	Evidence of a direct link to the event; not simply accidental	Evidence that it contributed to the event's direction and intensity	Evidence that the event would have been less likely if the factor was missing
Cause: ❏ Immediate ❏ Underlying			
Cause: ❏ Immediate ❏ Underlying			
Cause: ❏ Immediate ❏ Underlying			

The most important contributing factors:
Reasons:

1.

2.

3.

Blackline Master #4.4

	Outstanding	Very good	Competent	Satisfactory	In progress
Identifies plausible causes	Identifies a comprehensive list of possible causes, including less obvious immediate and underlying causes.	Identifies the most important causes, including a few less obvious immediate and underlying causes.	Identifies most of the important causes, including both immediate and underlying causes.	Identifies some important causes, but others may be omitted or are implausible.	Identifies very few plausible causes.
Comments/reasons for rating:					
Distinguishes immediate and underlying causes	Consistently and accurately distinguishes immediate and underlying causes.	In almost all cases, accurately distinguishes immediate and underlying causes.	In most cases, accurately distinguishes immediate and underlying causes.	Often misidentifies immediate and underlying causes.	Consistently misidentifies immediate and underlying causes.
Comments/reasons for rating:					
Identifies relevant evidence for each cause	Consistently identifies relevant, accurate, and substantial evidence about each cause's effect on the event.	Generally identifies relevant, accurate, and substantial evidence about each cause's effect.	Identifies relevant and accurate evidence about each cause's effect, but key pieces of evidence are overlooked.	Identifies some relevant and accurate evidence about each cause's effect. Often evidence is irrelevant or key evidence is omitted.	Identifies very little relevant and accurate evidence about each cause's effect on the event for any criteria.
Comments/reasons for rating:					

Justifies assigned rating	The assigned rating for each cause is highly plausible and clearly justified by the reasons provided.	Generally, the assigned rating for each cause is clearly plausible and justified by the reasons provided.	Often, the assigned rating for each cause is plausible and somewhat justified by the reasons provided.	Often the assigned rating for each cause is somewhat plausible, but barely justified by the reasons provided.	With few exceptions, the assigned rating for each cause is implausible and not justified by the reasons provided.
Comments/reasons for rating:					

5.
Identifying consequences

Critical tasks

A. Identify the obvious and less obvious direct and indirect consequences resulting from the event for the featured group(s).

B. Rate the severity of the collective impact on the featured group(s) in each of the following categories: political, social, economic, and emotional/psychological.

Overview

In this two-part challenge, students identify and assess the direct and indirect consequences of a historic event for a featured group. Students learn to recognize when something is the consequence of a prior event, and to distinguish consequences that follow directly from an event from those that are indirect. Students create a web of effects to illustrate the direct and indirect consequences resulting from an event in their own lives. They then turn their attention to the consequences of an assigned historical injustice. Using sources provided in the Righting Canada's Wrongs series, students gather information about various direct and indirect consequences. They classify the consequences for the featured group into four categories: political, social, economic, and psychological/emotional. Finally, students rate the severity of the impact of each category of consequence.

Pre-planning

Select the featured event

Prior to introducing the topic to students, determine which injustice (or injustices) featured in the Righting Canada's Wrongs series you wish to explore. Consult the *Key topics and references to Righting Canada's Wrongs texts* (page 103) for the relevant pages in the publication(s) that students might consult when identifying consequences.

Session One: What Are Consequences?

▶ Distinguish "consequence" from "afterward event"

Inform students that a consequence is a result or effect of an action or condition. Explain that just because an event occurred after another event does not mean that the subsequent event is a consequence of the first event. To qualify as a consequence, the second event must be a result of or be caused by the earlier event. For example, if a teenager left the house angry after having a dispute with her boyfriend and then got in a car accident, it is uncertain whether the car accident was a consequence of the quarrel. We would need to determine whether the accident simply happened after the fight, or whether the fight distracted or upset the girlfriend in such a way as to contribute to the accident.

▶ Using evidence to determine consequence

When determining the consequences of an event or action, it is important to provide evidence that links one event to another. For example, to say that the accident was a consequence of teenage angst, there would need to be evidence that the argument—not the road conditions, visibility, or speed the car was travelling—was a factor in the accident. Provide students with a specified action (e.g., a teacher walks into the classroom) and invite students to suggest all the possible events that may follow (e.g., students become silent, one student sneezes, a noise is heard from outside the classroom, several students start reading their textbooks). Ask students to suggest the kind of evidence that would be required to determine whether or not the follow-up events were a consequence of the initial action. For example, we would need evidence about the reasons why students stopped talking to connect it to the teacher's arrival. Is there evidence that they even noticed the teacher? Were whispers heard among students to keep quiet because the teacher had arrived?

▶ Explain direct and indirect consequences

Explain that an event may have multiple causes with different degrees of influence. Returning to the example of the car accident, suggest that it may be possible for there to be a trail of consequences from the dispute that led to the accident. Invite students to speculate on the range of possible events that resulted from the fight (e.g., the driver was angered by the fight, called her mother to complain, was distracted while talking on the phone, and in so doing missed the turn in the road and smashed into a tree). Record these in a list on the board. Invite students to draw the links from the fight to the subsequent accident. The initial consequence of the fight (getting mad) is the direct consequence. The rest of the events are indirect consequences. Explain the following terms:

- *Direct consequences* are the immediate results of a situation (e.g., bleeding is a direct consequence of cutting a finger, feeling cold is a direct consequence of going outside in the winter).

- *Indirect consequences* emerge as a result of a direct consequence and of other indirect consequences. For example, staining one's shirt with blood is an indirect consequence of cutting a finger. If a man was denied entry to a fancy restaurant because of his bloody shirt, this result would also be an indirect consequence of cutting his finger.

Apply the concepts to their own lives

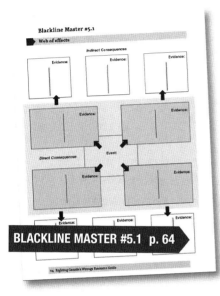

BLACKLINE MASTER #5.1 p. 64

Invite students to choose an important event that happened in their lives. Distribute a copy of *Web of effects* (Blackline Master #5.1) to each student or group of students. Invite them to identify several direct consequences of that important event, and for each direct consequence to think of several indirect consequences. In exploring the consequences of the initial event, remind students that events often have unintended consequences, and while we can identify some consequences, it may take years or even a lifetime to reveal others. Encourage students to provide evidence that supports any link connecting the suggested direct consequences with the initial action, and evidence to link the suggested indirect consequences to each other.

Self-assess the web of personal consequences

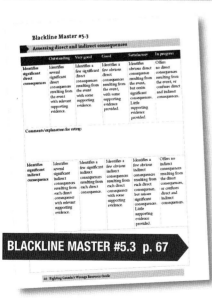

BLACKLINE MASTER #5.3 p. 67

Distribute a copy of the rubric found on *Assessing direct and indirect consequences* (Blackline Master #5.3). Ask each student working in pairs to review the completed copy of Blackline Master #5.1 in light of the criteria described in the rubric. Review any issues that students may not have understood.

View video on cause and consequence

OPTIONAL: Invite students to watch the short Take 2 video on *Cause and consequence* prepared by The Critical Thinking Consortium. Discuss the examples and the factors explained in the video.

 http://tinyurl.com/rcwthinkingabouthistory

Introduce the featured injustice

Inform students that they will now explore the consequences of an injustice committed against a featured group. They will examine historical evidence from various primary and secondary sources in order to draw conclusions about the breadth, depth, and duration of the impact of the injustice. Assign students individually or in groups to one of the injustices featured in the Righting Canada's Wrongs series.

Provide historical context

Ensure that students understand the historical context for the assigned injustice by inviting them to read and discuss the introductory pages of the relevant book in the Righting Canada's Wrongs series. Alternatively, ask students to share information they already know about the incident.

Identifying the consequence of the featured event

Distribute another copy of *Web of effects* (Blackline Master #5.1) to each student or team of students. Invite students to work through the sources on the relevant pages from Righting Canada's Wrongs, and to record the direct and indirect consequences on Blackline Master #1. Remind students to ignore subsequent events that may have occurred after an event but are not consequences of the event. Encourage students to recognize that indirect consequences can give rise to further consequences. The important point is not to correctly label every consequence but to understand that a particular event can have ripple effects throughout society over time.

Share preliminary findings

When students have identified most of the important direct and indirect consequences, arrange for them to discuss their findings with one or more colleagues. Encourage students to add any important consequences that they had not previously identified.

Evaluate the web of effect

Assess each student's identification of the indirect and direct consequences reported on *Web of effects* (Blackline Master #5.1) using the rubric found on *Assessing direct and indirect consequences* (Blackline Master #5.3). Encourage students to add to their web of consequences based on the assessment feedback.

Session Two: Severity of Consequences

▶ Introduce various kinds of consequences

Explain to students that events can have differentiated consequences. These can vary in the political, social, economic, and emotional/psychological ramifications. Provide the following definitions:

Political: Relating to or concerned with their rights and freedoms as citizens and their involvement with or influence by government and the legal system.

Social: Relating to the quality of interaction with others and the ability to take part in daily events involving others.

Economic: Relating to ability and conditions for work and to earn and enjoy a livelihood.

Psychological/emotional: Relating to the mental wellbeing or feelings and emotions of persons.

Offer a few sample consequences (e.g., people lose their homes, are denied access to university, lose the right to vote, feel like they don't belong, develop a stronger bond with their friends). Ask students to identify the category within which each consequence falls. Remind students that some consequences may affect more than one category. Advise students when this occurs to select the category that best represents the consequence. Ask students to suggest indirect consequences that might result from these consequences (e.g., the loss of opportunity to go to university may have economic consequences—loss of earning power—and emotional consequences—increased sense of personal frustration).

▶ Consider the severity of consequence

Explain to students that not all consequences have an equivalent impact; they can vary in their severity. When considering the impact of the consequences, invite students to consider three criteria:

Depth: How deeply felt or profound were the consequences?

Breadth: How widespread were their impact?

Duration: How long-lasting were the consequences?

Share a few examples of the consequences that students identified and discuss the depth, breadth, and duration of each.

Categorize and rate the consequences

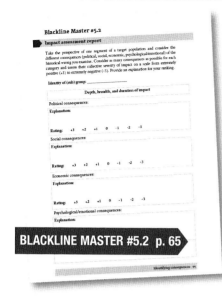

BLACKLINE MASTER #5.2 p. 65

Distribute a copy of *Impact assessment report* (Blackline Master #5.2). Invite students to categorize the consequences identified in their study of historical wrongs into the four categories listed on the left side of the page. Encourage students to identify as many as five consequences for each category. Ask students to assess the collective severity of the positive or negative impact of each category of consequence on a scale from extremely positive (+3) to extremely negative (-3). If needed, direct students back to the primary and secondary sources to collect evidence to support their ratings.

Share conclusions

Place students into groups of three or four and invite them to share their answers. Ask them to indicate which of the consequences were the most severe, and explain why. Invite students to share their responses with the rest of the class.

Evaluate the impact report

BLACKLINE MASTER #5.4 p. 68

Assess each student's evidence and rating for the impact of the consequences reported on *Impact assessment report* (Blackline Master #5.2). Use the rubric found on *Assessing the impact assessment* (Blackline Master #5.4).

Blackline Master #5.1

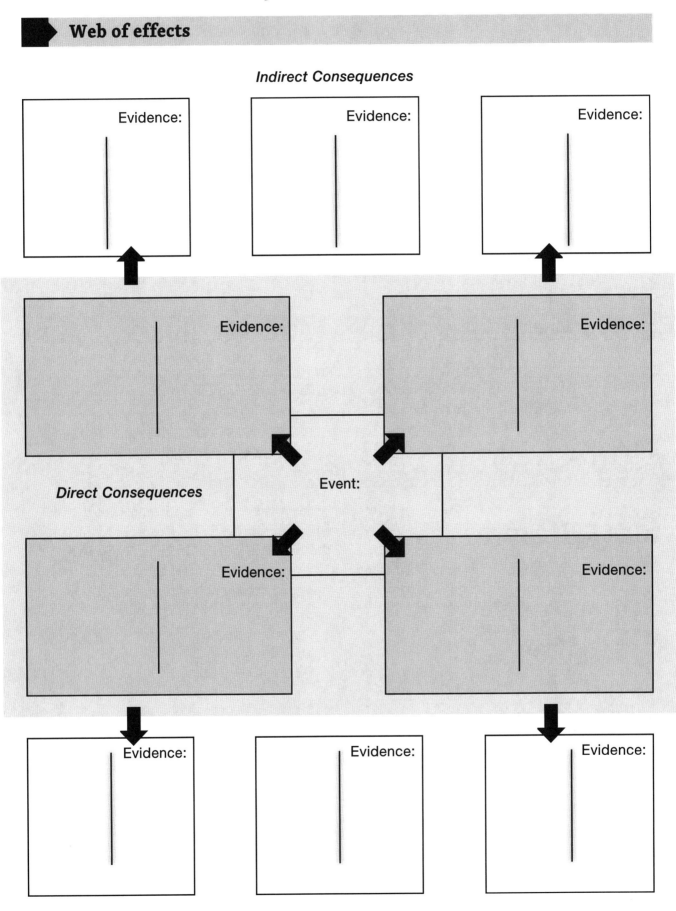

Indirect Consequences

Evidence:

Evidence:

Evidence:

Evidence:

Evidence:

Direct Consequences

Event:

Evidence:

Evidence:

Evidence:

Evidence:

Evidence:

Blackline Master #5.2

Impact assessment report

Take the perspective of one segment of a target population and consider the different consequences (political, social, economic, psychological/emotional) of the historical wrong you examine. Consider as many consequences as possible for each category and assess their collective severity of impact on a scale from extremely positive (+3) to extremely negative (-3). Provide an explanation for your ranking.

Identity of (sub) group: _____

	Depth, breadth, and duration of impact

Political consequences:

Explanation:

Rating: +3   +2   +1   0   -1   -2   -3

Social consequences:

Explanation:

Rating: +3   +2   +1   0   -1   -2   -3

Economic consequences:

Explanation:

Rating: +3   +2   +1   0   -1   -2   -3

Psychological/emotional consequences:

Explanation:

Rating: +3   +2   +1   0   -1   -2   -3

Overall Impact (considering evidence from all categories):

Blackline Master #5.3

Assessing direct and indirect consequences

	Outstanding	Very good	Good	Satisfactory	In progress
Identifies significant direct consequences	Identifies several significant direct consequences resulting from the event with relevant supporting evidence.	Identifies a few significant direct consequences resulting from the event with some supporting evidence.	Identifies a few obvious direct consequences resulting from the event, with some supporting evidence provided.	Identifies obvious direct consequence resulting from the event, but omits significant consequences. Little supporting evidence provided.	Offers no direct consequences resulting from the event, or confuses direct and indirect consequences.
Comments/explanation for rating:					
Identifies significant indirect consequence	Identifies several significant indirect consequences resulting from each direct consequence with relevant supporting evidence.	Identifies a few significant indirect consequences resulting from each direct consequence.	Identifies a few obvious indirect consequences resulting from each direct consequence with some supporting evidence.	Identifies a few obvious indirect consequences resulting from each direct consequence, but misses significant consequences. Little supporting evidence provided.	Offers no indirect consequences resulting from the direct consequences, or confuses direct and indirect consequences.
Comments/explanation for rating:					

Blackline Master #5.4

► Assessing the impact assessment

	Outstanding	Very good	Good	Satisfactory	In progress
Identifies relevant and important consequences for each category	Identifies several relevant and important consequences for each category.	Identifies several relevant and important consequences for most categories.	Identifies several consequences for most categories, but misses some important consequences.	Identifies a few obvious consequences for most categories, but misses the significant consequences.	Identifies very few consequences and often classifies them into inappropriate categories.
Comments/explanation for rating:					
Supports with accurate, relevant, and detailed evidence	Provides accurate and detailed evidence for the depth, breadth, and duration of impact for most of the identified consequences.	Provides generally accurate evidence for the depth, breadth, and duration of impact for most of the identified consequences.	Provides generally accurate evidence of impact for many of the identified consequences.	Provides evidence of impact for many of the identified consequences, but some evidence is inaccurate or exaggerated.	Provides very little evidence of impact for any of the identified consequences.
Comments/explanation for rating:					
Offers plausible ratings	Provides highly plausible ratings for each category.	Provides plausible ratings for each category.	Provides generally plausible ratings for most categories.	Provides plausible ratings for some categories, but not all.	Provides implausible ratings.
Comments/explanation for rating:					

6.
Offering ethical assessments

Critical task

Write a letter to a public official assessing the adequacy of the official response to a specified historic injustice.

Overview

In this challenge, students consider the overall adequacy of an official government response to a specific historical injustice documented in the Righting Canada's Wrongs series. First, students explore a contemporary school-related scenario to learn about criteria for judging the adequacy of a response to a legally-sanctioned but unjust act. Students then gather evidence from the Righting Canada's Wrongs series on the nature and consequences of the unjust treatment of an assigned historic group. Next, students investigate the official government's reactions and consider the arguments for and against the adequacy of that response. Finally, students prepare a letter outlining the consequences of the injustice and explaining whether or not the overall government's response was adequate.

Pre-planning

Select the featured event

Prior to introducing the topic to students, determine which injustice (or injustices) featured in the Righting Canada's Wrongs series you wish to explore. Consult the *Key topics and references to Righting Canada's Wrongs texts* (page 103) for the relevant pages in the publication(s) that students might consult when learning about the injustice and the government response to the injustice.

Present the sample scenario

BLACKLINE MASTER #6.1 p. 74

Distribute a copy of *Falsely accused* (Blackline Master #6.1) to each student or pair of students. As a class, read the fictional scenario about a youth who is punished for bringing pills to school that were incorrectly identified as illegal drugs. Ask students to express their opinions on whether the principal's response to the false accusation was adequate or not.

Discuss criteria for an adequate response

Individually or in groups, ask students to share the factors they considered when judging the adequacy of the principal's response. Invite students to compare the factors they used with the following criteria:

Sincere and full admission: acknowledges the mistakes and, where warranted, exposes any intentional wrongdoing;

Appropriate support: includes appropriate assistance and/or compensation for the negative experiences and consequences for the victims and their families and ancestors;

Prevention potential: response helps to build public awareness and avoid future injustices;

Fair consideration: response fairly respects the legitimate interests of all affected parties—doesn't create new victims or ignore old ones.

Critique the principal's response

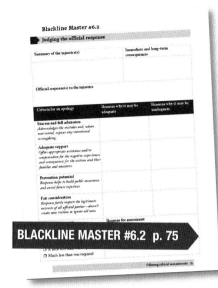

Blackline Master #6.2

Judging the official response

BLACKLINE MASTER #6.2 p. 75

Ask students to consider the difference between an official and unofficial response. Encourage them to consider the following distinction: an official response takes place within parliament in the House of Commons. An unofficial response is considered to be one that is given outside of parliament, even if it is delivered by the prime minister. Have students consider the importance of a response that takes place through the organs of government and speaks on behalf of the entire nation.

Distribute copies of *Judging the official response* (Blackline Master #6.2) and invite students to assemble reasons for and against the adequacy of the principal's response in light of the four criteria presented on the previous page. Place a copy on an overhead or digital projection and invite students to present their reasons supported with evidence from the scenario. Complete the overhead transparency as a class. Finally, ask students individually to rate the adequacy of the principal's response on a scale from "much more than required" to "much less than required." Ask students to indicate their conclusions with a show of hands. Discuss the varying reasons supporting different students' conclusions.

Introduce ethical judgments in history

Explain to students that in history we are often called upon to make ethical judgments of the appropriateness of the actions of governments and public officials. This was just what students did in the previous task when they judged whether the principal's response was adequate or not.

View video on ethical judgment

OPTIONAL: Invite students to watch the short Take 2 video on *Ethical judgment* prepared by The Critical Thinking Consortium. Discuss the examples and the factors explained in the video.

 http://tinyurl.com/rcwthinkingabouthistory

Introduce the featured injustice

Inform students that they will now explore the adequacy of the government response to an injustice. They will examine historical evidence from various primary and secondary sources to draw conclusions about the nature of the injustice and the impact on the people affected. Assign students individually or in groups to one of the injustices featured in the Righting Canada's Wrongs series.

Provide historical context

Ensure that students understand the historical context for the assigned injustice by inviting them to read and discuss the introductory pages of the relevant book in the Righting Canada's Wrongs series. Alternatively, ask students to share information they already know about the incident.

Find evidence about the event

Provide students with another copy of *Judging the official response* (Blackline Master #6.2) to use while researching their assigned injustice. Direct students to the relevant pages in the Righting Canada's Wrongs series to learn about the nature of the injustice, its consequences for the featured group, and the government's responses at the time and later on. Encourage students to look for evidence that supports and challenges the adequacy of the government's response on each of the identified criteria. Instruct them to come to a final conclusion about the response, ranging from "much more than was required" to "much less than was required," and to identify the three most compelling reasons for this judgment.

Session Two: Assessing Government Response

▶ Share preliminary findings

When students have completed Blackline Master #6.2, arrange for them to share their summary of the consequences of the injustice, the nature of the government's response, and the reasons for and against judging the response as adequate. Encourage students to add additional reasons that they had not previously identified and, if appropriate, to revise their overall assessment of the official response.

▶ Write a letter of appreciation or recommendation

After students have reviewed their reasons and overall assessments, inform them that they are to draft a letter to a relevant level of government that either (1) expresses appreciation and explains why the government response is adequate or (2) explains the inadequacy of the response and offers recommendations on the actions required to make proper amends.

▶ Assess the letter to the government

BLACKLINE MASTER #6.3 p. 76

Using the rubric found in *Assessing the ethical judgment* (Blackline Master #6.3), evaluate students' ability to judge the adequacy of the response to the injustice as reflected in students' completed copies of Blackline Master #6.1 and their letters to the governmental officials.

Blackline Master #6.1

Marcus had a terrible headache before school one day, but he didn't want to miss an important science class, so he took two acetaminophen pills. His mother placed a handful of pills in a plastic bag to take to school in case his headache continued. When Marcus arrived at school, he opened his locker and began to place the bag of pills inside it. Just at this moment, a teacher walked by. He immediately reported to the school principal, Mrs. Green, that he had seen Marcus at his locker with a bag of pills.

Mrs. Green went to Marcus's classroom, demanded that he gather all of his things, and escorted him roughly to her office. Once in the office, Mrs. Green informed Marcus that school authorities had forced open his locker and found a bag of illegal drugs inside. Marcus explained that they were pills for his headache. The principal was unconvinced, suggesting instead that Marcus had brought the pills to school for the purpose of selling them to other students. She suspended Marcus from school and informed his parents and the police.

When the police arrived, they handcuffed and escorted Marcus through the crowded hallways to the police car. He was detained overnight in jail and missed a week of classes because of the principal's suspension. News of his arrest spread throughout the community. The local newspaper contained an article on illegal drugs in schools and mentioned Marcus by name.

When the test results finally arrived, they revealed that the drugs were not illegal, but common headache medication. Upon learning of this development, Mrs. Green sent a letter to Marcus's home apologizing for the misunderstanding, and suggesting that he be more careful in future about bringing suspicious-looking drugs to school without a note from his parents.

Blackline Master #6.2

Judging the official response

Summary of the injustice(s)	Immediate and long-term consequences

Official response(s) to the injustice

Criteria for an apology	Reasons why it may be adequate	Reasons why it may be inadequate
Sincere and full admission *Acknowledges the mistakes and, where warranted, exposes any intentional wrongdoing.*		
Adequate support *Offers appropriate assistance and/or compensation for the negative experiences and consequences for the victims and their families and ancestors.*		
Prevention potential *Response helps to build public awareness and avoid future injustices.*		
Fair consideration *Response fairly respects the legitimate interests of all affected parties—doesn't create new victims or ignore old ones.*		

Overall assessment	Reasons for assessment
❏ Much more than was required	1.
❏ A little more than was required	2.
❏ Exactly what was required	
❏ A little less than was required	3.
❏ Much less than was required	

Blackline Master #6.3

	Outstanding	Very good	Competent	Satisfactory	In progress
Relevant and important consequences	Identifies many relevant and important consequences of the injustice.	Identifies many relevant consequences of the injustice.	Identifies some relevant consequences of the injustice.	Identifies a few of the relevant consequences of the injustice.	Identifies almost no relevant consequences of the injustice.
Comments/explanation for rating:					
Reasons for and against	For each of the criteria, identifies and explains thoughtful reasons for and against the adequacy of the official response to the injustice.	For most of the criteria, identifies generally thoughtful reasons for and against the adequacy of the official response to the injustice.	For most of the criteria, identifies and explains reasons for and against the adequacy of the official response; but some thoughtful reasons are missing.	For some of the criteria, identifies and explains reasons for and against the adequacy of the official response; but important reasons are missing.	Identifies and explains almost no thoughtful reasons for and against the adequacy of the official response.
Comments/explanation for rating:					
Justified ethical judgment	The ethical judgment is very reasonable and clearly justified by the reasons provided.	The ethical judgment is reasonable and well justified by the reasons provided.	The ethical judgment is reasonable and somewhat justified by the reasons provided.	The ethical judgment is reasonable but weakly justified by the reasons provided.	The ethical judgment is not reasonable.
Comments/explanation for rating:					

7.
Determining historical significance

Critical tasks

A. Identify the historically significant aspects or dimensions of your assigned event.

B. Design a visual commemorative piece featuring the most significant aspects of the historical injustice.

Overview

In this two-part challenge, students learn about the historical significance of legally sanctioned injustices featured in the Righting Canada's Wrongs series. Students are introduced to the concept of historical significance using events from their own lives. Next, students learn about the historical significance of one of the historical injustices featured in the series Righting Canada's Wrongs. Based on their analysis of primary and secondary sources, students decide which aspects or dimensions of the injustice are the most historically significant. Next, students are introduced to criteria for an effective commemoration. Students create a draft design for a commemoration of the most significant aspects of the injustice studied. Based on peer feedback, students revise their designs prior to sharing them with the rest of the class.

Pre-planning

Select the featured event

Prior to introducing the topic to students, determine which injustice (or injustices) featured in the Righting Canada's Wrongs series you wish to explore. Consult the *Key topics and references to Righting Canada's Wrongs texts* (page 103) for the suggested pages in each publication that students might consult for information about the event's historical significance.

Session One: Understanding Significance

Introduce the concept of significance

Ask students to write histories of their lives in ten bullet points or less. After students have finished their life histories, ask for volunteers to share their histories with the rest of the class. Explain to students that in the process of writing their life histories they made judgments about significance—what was important to include and what was not. Invite students to review the ten events on their lists and ask them to consider how they decided on the events to include and the ones to ignore. Create a chart, like the following, to record various suggested events and the reasons for their importance.

Sample event	Significance of the event
I moved from another country	*Turning point, life altering (consequences and symbolic of a new chapter)*
Death of my grandfather	*Affected the entire family (prominent at the time, scale of impact, deeply felt)*
I met Adam, who was my best friend throughout elementary school	*First met my best friend who I had stayed close to for years (consequences)*
Got caught stealing	*Taught me a lesson that I won't forget (symbolic, legacy)*

Introduce criteria for significance

Draw students' attention to the reasons offered for an event's significance by asking them to rank the three most important events from their list in order of importance. Implicit in these reasons are criteria for deciding about historical significance (e.g., coming to a Canada came to symbolize a new era in a student's life). Explain that the criteria for personal significance are similar to those for historical significance, except historical significance refers to a broader assessment beyond a single individual's concerns. Invite students to draw parallels between their reasons for ranking their own significant events and the following criteria for historical significance:

Scale of the incident—the profile of the event at the time:

- *Prominence at the time:* Was the event noticed by many or few people?

- *Duration:* Did the event span a long or a short time?

Consequences of the event—the lingering impact after the event was over:

- *Magnitude of impact:* How deeply felt or profound were the effects of the event?

- *Scope of impact:* How widespread was its impact? Were many people or geographic areas affected? Did it reach across various aspects of life?

- *Lasting nature:* How long-lasting were the effects? Were the effects short-lived or did the event change the direction of subsequent events for a long time to come?

Historical legacy—what the event has come to mean within the collective memory:

- *Symbolic:* Has the event been memorialized in popular culture or professional history? Has it assumed an iconic status within a group or society?

- *Revealing:* Does it inform our understanding of history? Is it emblematic of a condition of a period in history?

Determine the significance of a personal event

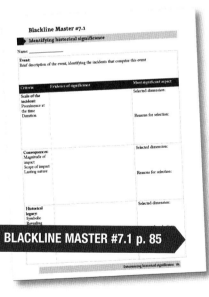

BLACKLINE MASTER #7.1 p. 85

Distribute a copy of *Identifying historical significance* (Blackline Master #7.1) to each student. Invite students to choose an event from their own lives and explain if and how the event is significant, given the three criteria discussed. In place of the third criteria—historical legacy—encourage students to consider how an event in their lives may be symbolic of a larger trend or pattern in their lives. You may choose to model how to complete Blackline Master #7.1 using a significant event from your own life. Request volunteers to present their explanations for the significance of their chosen event.

View video on historical significance

OPTIONAL: Invite students to watch the short Take 2 video on *Historical significance* prepared by The Critical Thinking Consortium. Discuss the examples and the factors explained in this video.

 http://tinyurl.com/rcwthinkingabouthistory

Introduce the featured injustice

Inform students that they will now explore the significance of an injustice committed against a featured group. They will examine historical evidence from various primary and secondary sources to draw conclusions about the scale, consequences, and historical legacy of the injustice. Assign students individually or in groups to look at one of the communities affected by an injustice featured in the Righting Canada's Wrongs series. Remind students that within an affected community, there are often sub-groups whose experiences may differ. For example, children were often oblivious to some of the hardships of internment suffered by their parents; mothers were faced with a disproportionate burden when their husbands were taken away.

Provide historical context

Ensure that students understand the historical context for the assigned injustice by inviting them to read and discuss the introductory pages of the relevant book in the Righting Canada's Wrongs series. Alternatively, ask students to share information they already know about the incident.

Gather evidence of historical significance

Distribute another copy of *Identifying historical significance* (Blackline Master #7.1) to each student. Explain that students are to examine the primary and secondary sources on the identified pages in the Righting Canada's Wrongs series. They are to look for information about the historical injustice and its scale, consequences, and historical legacy. Direct students, working individually or in pairs, to record this information in the "Evidence of significance" column of Blackline Master #7.1. Arrange for students to share their findings about the significance of the assigned event with other students.

Session Two: Commemorations

Judge the most significant aspects

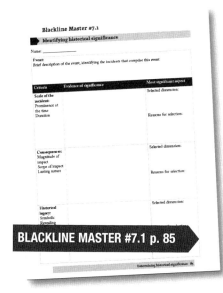

BLACKLINE MASTER #7.1 p. 85

When students have gathered and shared information about the event, invite them to consider which aspects of the injustice are most significant. For each of the three criteria for significance (scale, consequences and historical legacy), ask students to identify one most significant dimension. For example, when considering the scale of the incident, students might weigh the impact at the time of the seizure of property, conditions of internment, or the breadth of the operation. Direct students to identify their choices and provide supporting reasons in the "Most significant aspect" column of Blackline Master #7.1.

Evaluate conclusions about significance

Use the rubric found on *Assessing the significant aspects* (Blackline Master #7.2) to evaluate students' evidence and conclusions about the significant aspects of their assigned event as recorded on Blackline Master #7.1. Encourage students to add to or revise their evidence and conclusions based on the assessment feedback.

Introduce the idea of a commemoration

BLACKLINE MASTER #7.5 p. 90

Explain to students that their task is to design a powerful commemoration that features the most significant aspect(s) of the injustice they investigated. Invite students to share examples of commemorations of historical people or events they are familiar with (e.g., cenotaph war memorials, statues, museum exhibits, educational centres, commemorative coins). Ask them to consider the purpose of a commemoration.

Introduce criteria for an effective commemoration

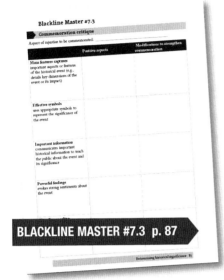

BLACKLINE MASTER #7.3 p. 87

Display various easily recognizable commemorations found in *Sample commemorations* (Blackline Master #7.5). Ask students to identify the characteristics that make commemorations powerful. Lead a group discussion on key criteria for an effective commemoration, or present students with the following list:

- captures the main features of the historical event (e.g., details key aspects of the event or its impact);

- uses effective symbols to represent the significance of the event (representative of the group/action, easily identifiable as relating to the event);

- introduces important historical information about the event for the uninitiated or uneducated, i.e. teaches about the event itself and the significance of the event;

- evokes strong feelings of the event or contains iconic images (e.g., prompts vivid images of the event and its lasting impact);

- is visually effective (e.g., composition, texture, and use of colour effectively reflect the injustice).

Critique sample commemorations

Distribute a copy of *Commemoration critique* (Blackline Master #7.3) to each student. Display each of the sample commemorations. Assign each student a different commemoration to critique so that all the samples are examined. Direct students to identify a positive aspect and a possible improvement in relation to each criterion of an effective design. Arrange for students to share their comments with others on the effectiveness of their assigned commemoration.

Prepare commemorative design

Review the criteria for an effective design and explain to students that their task is to prepare a draft design of their commemoration that will be critiqued by other students before they finalize their design. As a class, brainstorm imaginative ways to commemorate events (e.g., coin, collage, museum exhibit, statue). Direct students to sketch a prototype of a suitable commemoration that features one or more significant aspects of the injustice they explored.

▶ Invite peer feedback on their commemorative prototypes

Distribute another copy of Blackline Master #7.3 to each student. Working in pairs, arrange for students to explain their design decisions and how each relates to the criteria for an effective commemoration. Each partner is to provide feedback on the positive aspects and possible improvements. Encourage students to revise their draft design in light of the peer feedback.

Session Three: Commemoration Presentations

Share final commemorations

Arrange for students to share their final versions with the rest of the class. Invite the class to discuss how well they capture the event's significance. Alternatively, distribute several examples to teams of students, and invite each team to identify the events, and select the most powerful commemoration for each of the injustices studied. Consider posting these commemorations in a prominent place in the classroom or school.

Evaluate the commemorations

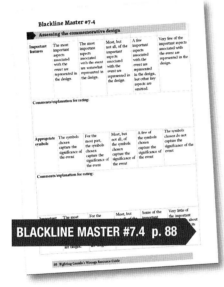

BLACKLINE MASTER #7.4 p. 88

Assess the final versions of students' commemorative designs using the rubric found in *Assessing the commemorative design* (Blackline Master #7.4).

Extension

Encourage students to explain the significance of their event in terms of an overarching metaphor. Explain that historians adopt different kinds of metaphors to help them conceptualize complex stories as possessing some kind of unity over centuries of time, thousands of locations, and millions of lives. History is sometimes characterized as a river, a tree, a labyrinth, or a circle. Metaphors for specific events in history can also be derived, and are useful tools for portraying complex stories in a simpler manner. For instance, the myth of David and Goliath can serve as a metaphor for many historical wars involving a large and a small power. Encourage students to develop short metaphorical statements to represent the significance of their assigned event.

Blackline Master #7.1

Identifying historical significance

Name: _____

Event: Brief description of the event, identifying the incidents that comprise this event		
Criteria	**Evidence of significance**	**Most significant aspect**
Scale of the incident: Prominence at the time Duration		Selected dimension: Reasons for selection:
Consequences: Magnitude of impact Scope of impact Lasting nature		Selected dimension: Reasons for selection:
Historical legacy: Symbolic Revealing		Selected dimension: Reasons for selection:

Blackline Master #7.2

	Outstanding	Very good	Competent	Satisfactory	In progress
Accurate, relevant, and comprehensive evidence	The information is accurate, clearly relevant, and comprehensive of the important facts for each criterion of significance.	The information is accurate, relevant, and includes the most important facts for each criterion.	The information is largely accurate, generally relevant, and includes many of the most important facts for each criterion.	The information is often accurate and relevant, and includes a few of the important facts for each criterion.	The information is often inaccurate or irrelevant and omits the most important facts.
Comments/explanation for rating:					
Justifiable selection of significant aspects	The selected significant aspects are highly justifiable given what historians know about the event.	The selected significant aspects are generally justifiable given what historians know about the event.	The selected most significant aspects are somewhat justifiable given what historians know about the event.	The selected most significant aspects include elements that are justifiable and others that are not justifiable.	The selected most significant aspects are not at all justifiable given what historians know about the event.
Comments/explanation for rating:					

Blackline Master #7.3

Aspect of injustice to be commemorated: _____

	Positive aspects	Modifications to strengthen commemoration
Main features captures important aspects or features of the historical event (e.g., details key dimensions of the event or its impact)		
Effective symbols uses appropriate symbols to represent the significance of the event		
Important information communicates important historical information to teach the public about the event and its significance		
Powerful feelings evokes strong sentiments about the event		
Visually appealing the display is arranged in an effective and appealing manner		

Blackline Master #7.4

	Outstanding	Very good	Competent	Satisfactory	Underdeveloped
Important features	The most important aspects associated with the event are represented in the design.	The most important aspects associated with the event are somewhat represented in the design.	Most, but not all, of the important aspects associated with the event are represented in the design.	A few important aspects associated with the event are represented in the design, but other key aspects are omitted.	Very few of the important aspects associated with the event are represented in the design.
Comments/explanation for rating:					
Appropriate symbols	The symbols chosen capture the significance of the event	For the most part, the symbols chosen capture the significance of the event	Most, but not all, of the symbols chosen capture the significance of the event	A few of the symbols chosen capture the significance of the event	The symbols chosen do not capture the significance of the event
Comments/explanation for rating:					

Important historical information	The most important information about the event and its significance are taught.	For the most part, information about the event and its significance are taught.	Most, but not all, of the information about the event and its significance are taught.	Some of the important information about the event and its significance are taught.	Very little of the important information about the event and its significance are taught.

Comments/explanation for rating:

Powerful feelings	The images powerfully evoke the significance of the event.	For the most part, the images vividly recreate the significance of the event.	Most, but not all, of the images vividly recreate the significance of the event.	A few images recreate the significance of the event, but key aspects are not powerfully represented.	The images do not recreate the significance of the event.

Comments/explanation for rating:

Visually appealing	The design is arranged in an especially effective and visually appealing manner.	The design is competently arranged and generally appealing.	Most of the design is competently arranged and somewhat appealing.	A few aspects of the design are arranged in an interesting and appealing way, but other aspects disrupt the effect.	The design appears very cluttered or otherwise unappealing.

Comments/explanation for rating:

Blackline Master #7.5

The Warsaw Ghetto Uprising was a 1943 Jewish revolt against the deportation of the remaining Jews in the ghetto to extermination camps. The three-week uprising was eventually crushed by a systematic destruction of the buildings and their occupants. www.en.wikipedia.org/wiki/Warsaw_Ghetto_Uprising

source: www.coinnews.net/2008/04/15/warsaw-ghetto-uprising-zloty-coins-released-by-poland-4032

Image © National Bank of Poland Images

Killing Fields commemoration: Cambodia

The Killing Fields refers to the systematic murder of Cambodian civilians by the Khmer Rouge regime between 1975 and 1979. It is estimated that a quarter of the country's population was killed by the Khmer Rouge. www.en.wikipedia.org/wiki/Killing_Fields

Image © Paul Mannix

Symbolic interpretation of the history of Chinese immigrants by sculptor Peter Sawatsky

Chinese immigrants to Canada faced systematic discrimination and racism in the early twentieth century. Their contribution and eventual acceptance into Canadian society mirrors Canada's shift to multiculturalism.
www.en.wikipedia.org/wiki/History_of_Chinese_immigration_to_Canada

Image © Gordon Goldsborough

First World War Memorial, Ottawa

The First World War (1914–1918) was a turning point in Canadian identity and independence. Canada emerges as a formidable fighting power that is recognized internationally.
www.en.wikipedia.org/wiki/Military_history_of_Canada_during_World_War_I

Image © iStock/Andre Nantel

Ukrainian internment

The Ukrainian internment refers to the decision by the Canadian government to place Ukrainian and Austro-Hungarian men, women, and children in detention and work camps during the First World War. While fear of enemy aliens during wartime is widely cited as the explanation for the internment, the camps continued to operate two years after the war's end. http://en.wikipedia.org/wiki/Ukrainian_Canadian_internment

Image © Canadian First World War Internment Recognition Fund

Holocaust Memorial, Miami, Florida

The Holocaust refers to the systemic extermination of European Jewry and the mass murder of Roma, homosexuals, Jehovah's Witnesses, and political dissidents by Nazi Germany and its collaborators between 1941 and 1945. The industrial scale and efficiency of the killings led to the establishment of human rights laws. http://en.wikipedia.org/wiki/The_Holocaust

Image © iStock/Burcin Tuncer

Rwandan Genocide Memorial

The Rwandan genocide was the systematic slaughter of Rwandans of Tutsi descent by Hutu militants in 1994.
The evacuation of United Nations troops from Rwanda as the killings began reflects the indifference of the
international community at the time. http://en.wikipedia.org/wiki/Rwandan_Genocide

Image © Adam Jones

Teaching about racism

The following excerpts have been taken from: www.embracebc.ca/local/embracebc/ pdf/make_a_case_teachers_guide.pdf — "Make A Case Against Racism: A Guide for Teachers of Grades 4–7." *Lorimer additions are shown in italics.*

▶ Pre-teaching considerations related to anti-racism education

Racism is a topic that conjures up a range of thoughts and emotions. In approaching this topic, teachers may find it helpful to consider:

- how their own background and experience might affect their approach to the topic (those who have not personally witnessed or experienced racism may not be aware of its presence or of its impact on those who have);

- what their own thoughts and feelings are with respect to this subject;

- what generalizations or stereotypes they themselves may have harboured;

- what race-related power dynamics might exist in their classrooms (e.g., who might be experiencing racism—either in subtle ways, or through bullying, harassment, or intimidation);

- how best to create a safe learning environment where racism can be discussed in a constructive way.

Goodwill and professional judgment grounded in classroom management experience are important assets when approaching this topic. In addition, however, teachers may find it helpful to approach the discussion with:

- heightened sensitivity to the comfort levels of students who might have first-hand experience of racism;

- honest acknowledgment of their own limitations (e.g., not having personally experienced what it is like to be a target of racism);

- some familiarity with the terminology and concepts involved with anti-racism education (see the resources mentioned earlier in this Introduction and the Glossary included at the end of the resource);

- a clear sense of boundaries regarding forms of self-expression in the school environment (respecting students' needs and rights to self-expression and inclusion does **not** involve a validation of any or all opinions; self-expression that is hurtful or that can readily be construed as a perpetuation of oppression or injustice should not be a part of classroom discourse and should be immediately addressed).

It is hoped that teachers who have addressed these considerations will find that the students who may have experienced racism welcome a chance to have their reality acknowledged, placed in context, and discussed openly.

Introduce the concept of social responsibility. Ask students to brainstorm what they think this term means. Guide the discussion toward the following key elements:

- contributing to the classroom and school community;

- solving problems in a peaceful way;

- valuing diversity and defending human rights;

- exercising democratic rights and responsibilities.

Connect the concept of social responsibility to the following terms (see also the Glossary):

prejudice: explain to students that the underlying meaning of the word prejudice is to **prejudge**; discuss how they think prejudging (prejudice) and making broad generalizations about groups and/or individuals (stereotyping) lead to poor treatment of people.

discrimination: point out the fundamental unfairness and the limitations involved in treating people with disrespect on the basis of difference.

racism: point out the ways in which racism can adversely affect an entire community (e.g., limit access to opportunity, limit development of society's full potential, undermine members' sense of belonging). *For a very good discussion on racism, its meaning, and its impact on society, see www.canadaandtheworld.com/archive.html and click on **racism** in the drop-down box under Archives, then click on **Defining Racism**.*

Depending on the age and maturity levels of your students, you may consider extending discussion to include the term "hate crime" or the term "genocide" as an extreme form of systemic racism. You might also use current news articles to have students identify real-life examples of prejudice, stereotyping, discrimination, and racism, and indicate how/why these are hurtful. *Guide the discussion to help students understand how a belief in a stereotype or prejudice, without realizing it, can easily lead to discriminatory behaviour.*

A "prevailing attitude" is a historical and accepted stereotype that most people in a population accept. The prevailing attitude in the early twentieth century on the west coast of Canada was anti-Asian. J. Arthur Lower wrote about this in the following passage from Canada & The World, *Toronto: MacLean-Hunter, 1977. ISSN 0043-8170.*

Racists saw the hundreds of millions across the Pacific as an immigrant threat which could swamp the white settlers. Furthermore, said the racists, these people could not be assimilated (absorbed into society so that cultural differences could disappear) because of their colour, languages, clothes, religions, foods, and customs.

As people complained and politicians responded, laws were passed against Asian immigrants, including Japanese, Chinese, and Indian people. These racist laws were part of the "official" or "systemic" racism that Asian immigrants faced in Canada.

We also recommend the teaching resource material "Internment and Redress: The Japanese Canadian Experiencs" for the BC Ministry of Education. A sample can be found at www.japanesecanadianhistory.net/secondary_guide.htm and ordering information is available there.

Glossary

Definitions provided here are taken from the following document: Province of British Columbia. British Columbia Multicultural Advisory Council. *Strategic Framework for Action: A Strategy to Stimulate Joint Action on Multiculturalism and the Elimination of Racism in British Columbia*. Vancouver, 2005.

Anti-racism The practice of identifying, challenging, preventing, eliminating, and changing the values, structures, policies, programs, practices, and behaviours that perpetuate racism.

Bias An inclination or preference based on something other than facts or evidence.

Discrimination The practice or act of making distinctions between people on the basis of prejudicial attitudes and beliefs, which leads to the inequitable treatment of individuals or groups.

Diversity The variety of characteristics all persons possess that distinguish them as individuals and identify them as belonging to a group or groups. Diversity is a concept that includes notions of age, class, culture, ability, ethnicity, family, sex, language, place of origin, race, religion, and sexual orientation, as well as other characteristics that vary among people and groups within society.

Ethnicity A social and political term used by individuals and communities to define themselves and others. Specifically, "ethnicity" refers to a person's cultural background, including his or her language, origin, faith, and heritage. Ethnicity comprises the ideas, beliefs, values, and behaviour that are transmitted from one generation to the next. Ethnicity tends to be perceived in terms of common culture, history, language, or nationhood. Ethnicity and ethnic identity are interchangeable terms.

Hate An intense dislike of, and contempt for, another person or group of people.

Hate/Bias Crime A hate/bias crime is a criminal offence committed against a person or property, which is motivated by the suspect's hate, prejudice, or bias against an identifiable group based on race, national or ethnic origin, language, colour, religion, sex, age, mental or physical disability, sexual orientation, or any other similar factor (as defined in section 718.2 of the *Criminal Code of Canada*) (definition from *Hate/Bias Crime Pocket Guide*). Verbal intimidation, assault, and vandalism are the most commonly reported types of hate crimes.

Multiculturalism Refers to a society that recognizes, values, and promotes the contributions of the diverse cultural heritages and ancestries of all its people. A multicultural society is one that continually evolves and is strengthened by the contributions of its diverse peoples.

Prejudicial A preconceived idea or judgment toward a group, based on perceived ethnic or ancestral characteristics that result in a belief that members of that group are inferior.

Racial Discrimination As one of the many signatories to the International Convention on the Elimination of All Forms of Racism in 1969, Canada agreed to the following definition of racial discrimination found in Article 1: "Racial discrimination" shall mean any distinction, exclusion, restriction, or preference based on race, colour, descent, or national or ethnic origin, which has the purpose or effect of nullifying or impairing the recognition, enjoyment or exercise, on an equal footing, of human rights and fundamental freedoms in the political, social, cultural, or any other field of public life.

Racism A set of mistaken assumptions, opinions, and actions resulting from the belief that one group of people categorized by colour or ancestry is inherently superior to another. Racism may be present in organizational and institutional policies, programs, and practices, as well as in the attitudes and behaviour of individuals.

Stereotyping Refers to a belief that certain people are exactly the same, just because they have some things in common (such as skin colour, origin, ancestry, physical condition, habits, wealth or lack thereof, occupation, age, sexual orientation, etc.).

Key topics and references to Righting Canada's Wrongs texts

Each of the lessons in the first part of this resource can be used with any of the books in the Righting Canada's Wrongs series. In this part of the resource, you will find the page references and topics from each book in the series that correspond with a specific lesson. The following table of contents specifies where you can locate the relevant information for each book.

Japanese Canadian Internment in the Second World War

▶ Examining historical causation

A. Identify the various underlying and immediate causes of a particular event.

B. Determine the three most important contributing factors to the event.

▶ Key topics: *Japanese Canadian Internment in the Second World War*

In exploring the immediate and underlying causes related to the Japanese Canadian internment, the following events are most important:

1. Causes of Japanese immigration to Canada from 1877–1914: pp. 8–17.

   a. Push factors: rice riots, poverty and starvation, excessive taxation, immigration restrictions in other countries.

   b. Pull factors: promise of a better life, family who had already immigrated to Canada, promise of employment.

2. Causes of the government's decision to intern Japanese Canadians from 1942–1945: pp. 18–19, 28–85 (especially pages 70–81).

   a. Societal and government-sanctioned racism.

   b. Concern about the international threat to Canadian security.

   c. Concern about domestic security.

   d. War hysteria.

   e. Political advantage.

   f. Economic benefit.

3. Causes of the government's decision to acknowledge the injustice of Japanese Canadian internment: pp. 144–148.

   a. Pressure from national Japanese-Canadian community groups and other ethnic groups, unions, professional organizations, religious and cultural groups, and private citizens.

   b. Sincere regret about the violation of human rights during the war and commitment to create a society that ensures equality and justice for all.

   c. United States government decision to sign a redress bill with Japanese Americans.

   d. Political pressure and advantage.

Identifying consequences

A. Identify the obvious and less obvious direct and indirect consequences resulting from the historic injustice for the featured group(s).

B. Rate the severity of the collective impact on the featured group in each of the following categories: political, social, economic, psychological/emotional.

Key topics: *Japanese Canadian Internment in the Second World War*

1. Obvious and less obvious direct and indirect consequences of the Japanese Canadian internment:

    a. Direct consequences: pp. 82–123.

    b. Indirect consequences: pp. 124–151.

2. When determining the severity of the collective impact of the consequences of internment for Japanese Canadians, consider the following areas:

    a. Psychological and emotional consequences.

    b. Social and cultural consequences.

    c. Economic consequences.

    d. Political and legal consequences.

Tracking continuity and change

A. Identify the similarities and differences between the experiences of two groups or a single group over two time periods.

B. Identify the most important similarity and difference between the compared groups or time periods.

Key topics: *Japanese Canadian Internment in the Second World War*

When tracking continuity and change between the experiences of Japanese Canadians and one or more groups, consider the following topics:

1. Causes of Japanese Canadian internment: pp. 18–19, 28–85.

2. Internment experience for Japanese Canadians: pp. 72–137.

3. Racism experienced by Japanese Canadians prior to their internment: pp. 14–67.

4. Consequences of internment for Japanese Canadians: direct consequences pp. 82–123; indirect consequences: pp. 124–151.

5. Government acknowledgement and redress for Japanese Canadian internment: pp. 144–148.

When comparing a single group at two different time periods, consider the following topics:

1. Attitudes towards and treatment of Japanese Canadians before the war and during internment: pp. 14–59 (pre-war), pp. 68–138 (post-war).

2. Life in Canada for Japanese Canadians before and after internment: pp. 14–59 (pre-war), pp. 124–151 (post-war).

Offering ethical assessments

A. Write a letter to a public official assessing the adequacy of the official response to a specified historical injustice.

Key topics: *Japanese Canadian Internment in the Second World War*

Consider the following areas when assessing the adequacy of the official response of the federal government to Japanese Canadian internment:

1. Experiences during and consequences of Japanese Canadian internment: direct consequences pp. 82–123; indirect consequences: pp. 124–151.

2. Government response to Japanese Canadian internment: pp. 144–147.

Adopting historical perspectives

A. Draw historically plausible conclusions about the experiences and attitudes of a featured group regarding some aspect of a historical injustice.

B. Write a letter from the point of view of a teenage member of the group explaining the specified situation or event.

Key topics: *Japanese Canadian Internment in the Second World War*

Consider one or more of the following topics when adopting a historical perspective related to Japanese Canadian internment:

1. Japanese attitudes towards immigrating to Canada prior to internment: pp. 8–39.

2. Canadian attitudes towards Asian immigration prior to internment: pp. 16–35.

3. Degree to which nikkei maintained Japanese culture or accepted Canadian culture prior to internment: pp. 34–59.

4. Degree of inclusion/exclusion felt by people of Japanese descent prior to internment: pp. 18–59.

5. Nikkei attitudes towards the beginning of the Second World War: pp. 66–71.

6. Nikkei attitudes towards the restriction of their rights prior to internment in February 1942: pp. 72–79.

7. Daily life for a teenager in:

   Hastings Park: pp. 86–91.

   Road camps and prison camps: pp. 110–113.

   Internment camps: pp. 96–109, 114–115.

   Forced labour on the Prairies: pp. 116–119.

8. Nisei feelings about the fairness of internment: pp. 82–121.

9. Reasons offered by government officials and politicians to justify internment: pp. 68–81.

10. Nisei attitudes towards joining the Canadian war effort in 1945: pp. 122–123.

11. Attitudes towards the Canadian government's decision in 1945 to require Japanese Canadians either to resettle east of the Rockies or be deported to Japan: pp. 124–123.

12. Attitudes towards the federal government's official redress agreement, signed in 1988: pp. 144–151.

Determining historical significance

A. Identify the historically significant aspects or dimensions of your assigned event.

B. Design a commemorative piece (e.g., coin, collage, museum exhibit, statue, video, memorial epitaph, poem, song) featuring the most significant aspects of the historical injustice.

Key topics: *Japanese Canadian Internment in the Second World War*

When identifying historically significant aspects of the Japanese Canadian internment, consider the following criteria:

1. Recognition of internment at the time: pp. 72–95.

2. Consequences of internment: direct consequences pp. 82–123; indirect consequences: pp. 124–151.

3. Iconic status and insights about the past: pp. 144–151; how the Japanese Canadian internment has been memorialized by different groups: pp. 148-151.

Italian Canadian Internment in the Second World War

Examining historical causation

A. Identify the various underlying and immediate causes of a particular event.

B. Determine the three most important contributing factors to the event.

Key topics

In exploring the immediate and underlying causes related to the Italian Canadian internment, the following events are most important:

1. Causes of Italian immigration to Canada from the late 1800s to early 1900s

   a. Push factors: pp. 8–13 (poor crops, high rent for small parcels of land, unemployment, poverty, excessive taxation, limited job prospects).

   b. Pull factors: pp. 14-21 (job opportunities, adventure, testimonials from Italian immigrants already in Canada, promise of a better life, promise of free land, reunite family).

2. Causes of the government's decision to intern Italian Canadians from 1940–1945: pp. 44-53, 56-63.

   a. Societal and government-sanctioned racism: pp. 44-45.

   b. Canadian connections to Italian fascism: pp. 46-51.

   c. Canadian declaration of war on Italy: pp. 52-53.

   d. Concern about domestic security during the war: pp. 56-63.

▶ Identifying consequences

A. Identify the obvious and less obvious direct and indirect consequences resulting from the historic injustice for the featured group(s).

B. Rate the severity of the collective impact on the featured group in each of the following categories: political, social, economic, psychological/emotional.

▶ Key topics

1. Obvious and less obvious direct and indirect consequences of the Italian Canadian internment:

   a. Direct consequences: pp. 64-87.

   b. Indirect consequences: pp. 88-99.

2. When determining the severity of the collective impact of the consequences of internment for Italian Canadians, consider the following areas: pp. 64-103.

   a. Psychological and emotional consequences.

   b. Social and cultural consequences.

   c. Economic consequences.

   d. Political and legal consequences.

Tracking continuity and change

A. Identify the similarities and differences between the experiences of two groups or a single group over two time periods.

B. Identify the most important similarity and difference between the compared groups or time periods.

Key topics

When tracking continuity and change between the experiences of Italian Canadians and one or more groups, consider the following topics:

1. Causes of immigration: pp. 8-21.

2. Daily life in Canada prior to Internment: pp. 14-47.

3. Causes of Italian Canadian internment: pp. 44-53, 56-63.

4. Internment experiences for Italian Canadians: pp. 60-77.

5. Racism experienced by Italian Canadians prior to their internment: pp. 44-45.

6. Consequences of internment for Italian Canadians: direct consequences pp. 64-87; indirect consequences: pp. 88-99.

7. Government acknowledgement and redress for Italian Canadian internment: pp. 100–103.

When comparing a single group at two different time periods, consider the following topic:

1. Life in Canada for Italian Canadians before and after internment: pp. 14–59 (pre-internment), pp. 90-103 (post-internment).

▶ Offering ethical assessments

A. Write a letter to a public official assessing the adequacy of the official response to a specified historical injustice.

▶ Key topics

Consider the following areas when assessing the adequacy of the official response of the federal government to Italian Canadian internment:

1. Experiences during and consequences of Italian Canadian internment: direct consequences: pp. 60-87; indirect consequences: pp. 88-99.

2. Government response to Italian Canadian internment: pp. 100-103.

Adopting historical perspectives

A. Draw historically plausible conclusions about the experiences and attitudes of a featured group regarding some aspect of a historical injustice.

B. Write a letter from the point of view of a teenage member of the group explaining the specified situation or event.

Key topics

Consider one or more of the following topics when adopting a historical perspective related to Italian Canadian internment:

- Italian attitudes towards immigrating to Canada prior to internment: pp. 8–21.

- Life in Canada in the early twentieth century: pp. 22-23.

- Daily life in Canada for Italian immigrants prior to internment: pp. 24-51.

- Degree of inclusion/exclusion felt by people of Italian descent prior to internment: pp. 24-47.

- Italian Canadian attitudes towards Italian fascism: pp. 46–51.

- Italian Canadian attitudes towards supporting the Canadian war effort: pp. 52-55.

- Daily life for internees in:

a. Camp Petawawa and KP4W: pp. 68–71

b. Camp Ripples: pp. 72–77.

- Italian Canadian family life during World War II: pp. 64-67 and pp. 78-87.

- Life after internment for Italian Canadians: pp. 94-101.

- Attitudes towards the federal government's official response to internment: pp. 100-103.

Determining historical significance

A. Identify the historically significant aspects or dimensions of your assigned event.

B. Design a commemorative piece (e.g., coin, collage, museum exhibit, statue, video, memorial epitaph, poem, song) featuring the most significant aspects of the historical injustice.

Key topics

When identifying historically significant aspects of the Italian Canadian internment, consider the following criteria:

1. Recognition of internment at the time: pp. 52-67 and pp. 78-89.

2. Consequences of internment: direct consequences: pp. 64-87; indirect consequences: pp. 88-99.

3. Iconic status and insights about the past: pp. 100-101; how the Italian Canadian internment has been memorialized by different groups: pp. 102-103.

Author Biographies

Dr. Roland Case is executive director and co-founder of The Critical Thinking Consortium. He was a professor of Social Studies Education at Simon Fraser University. Roland has edited or written over 100 published works. Notable among these are *Understanding Judicial Reasoning* (Thompson Publishing, 1997), *The Anthology of Social Studies: Volume I and II* (Pacific Educational Press, 2008), and *Critical Challenges across the Curriculum*, the award-winning series of TC² teaching resources. In addition to his teaching career as an elementary school teacher and university professor, Roland has worked with many classroom teachers across Canada and in the United States, England, Israel, Russia, India, Finland, and Hong Kong to support the infusion of critical thinking. Roland is the 2006 recipient of CUFA's Distinguished Academics Career Achievement Award.

Ilan Danjoux is a recent PhD graduate that examined the predictive power of Middle East political cartoons. His forthcoming book on political cartoons and the Israeli Palestinian conflict is published by the University of Manchester Press. He has fifteen years of teaching experience and curriculum design at every level of education, ranging from preschool to Masters programs. Ilan helped develop York University's first online courses, operated an online education website, and designed online learning modules for the University of Leicester.

Lindsay Gibson is a PhD student in the Department of Curriculum and Pedagogy at the University of British Columbia, currently working on his dissertation proposal and research that will focus on teaching historical thinking. Lindsay is also involved with the Canada-wide Historical Thinking Project and is a member of the Graduate Committee for The History Education Network (THEN/HiER). He has taught social studies methods courses to pre-service teachers in the Bachelor of Education program at the University of British Columbia and the University of British Columbia Okanagan for the past three years. Lindsay taught secondary school history and social studies in Kelowna, BC for ten years and returned to the classroom part-time in the spring of 2012.

MARQUIS

Québec, Canada